Renaissance
Papers
2002

Renaissance Papers

2002

Editors
Christopher Cobb
M. Thomas Hester

❧

Published for
THE SOUTHEASTERN RENAISSANCE CONFERENCE
by
Camden House

THE SOUTHEASTERN RENAISSANCE CONFERENCE

2002 Officers

President: John N. Wall, North Carolina State University
Vice President: Boyd Berry, Virginia Commonwealth University
Secretary-Treasurer: Gerald Snare, Tulane University

Renaissance Papers 2002

ISBN 1-57113-051-9
ISSN 0584-4207

Published by:

Camden House
An imprint of Boydell & Brewer, Inc.
668 Mt. Hope Avenue, Rochester, NY 14620 USA

and of Boydell & Brewer Ltd.
P.O. Box 9, Woodbridge, Suffolk IP12 3DF, UK

TABLE OF CONTENTS

Poetry, Patronage, and Identity in the Dance of the
  Graces, Book VI of *The Faerie Queene*
  ALZADA TIPTON

The "Allurement of Liking" and the "Contentation of
  the Eyes": Decoding the Visual Culture of the
  Elizabethan Prodigy House
  JAMES M. SUTTON

Discovering Authorial Intention in the Manuscript
  Sequences of Donne's Holy Sonnets
  GARY STRINGER

RENAISSANCE PAPERS

read at the Annual Meeting
and to be published elsewhere

Christopher Hodgkins (University of North Carolina, Greensboro)
"The Vniversall Wheele of Things": Herbert, Daniel, and the
Augustinian Critique of Empire" will be published in his
forthcoming book *Reforming Empire: Protestant Colonialism and
Conscience in British Literature.*.

Renaissance Papers

A Selection of Papers
Submitted to the
Fifty-ninth Annual Meeting
April 5–6, 2002
North Carolina State University
Raleigh, North Carolina

Pastoral Community and the Hooks of Memory: The Mnemonic Landscape of Izaak Walton's *Compleat Angler* (1653)

ANNE E. MCILHANEY

THIS essay explores the prominence Walton gives in the *Compleat Angler* to the issue of memory—a prominence that has been overlooked in Walton scholarship, and that links the *Compleat Angler* not only with studies of mnemonics in the Renaissance, but also with studies of the role of memory in the politics of oppression. For, as critics have been observing for decades, the first edition of Walton's well-known fishing book appeared in 1653, during the Interregnum. Walton and his friends, many of whom were among the clergy dispossessed in those years, were Anglicans and Royalists, forced into exile or retired life. B. D. Greenslade and Jonquil Bevan have amply demonstrated that Walton had friends among the sequestered Anglican clergy (who corresponded among themselves about angling), and that the *Compleat Angler* can be read as a book of "consolation . . . for the dispossessed."[1] Walton's book includes a compelling, if implicit, political component: it promotes courteous verbal exchanges and extends comfort for dispossessed Anglicans in a disconcerting time for both Royalists and the nation at large.[2] But in addition to (and through) his use of dialogue to accomplish these aims, Walton

---

[1] Jonquil Bevan, *Izaak Walton's "The Compleat Angler": The Art of Recreation* (Sussex: Harvester, 1988), p. 28. See also B. D. Greenslade, "The Compleat Angler and the Sequestered Clergy," *RES* n.s. 5 (1954): 361-6.

[2] See especially Jonquil Bevan, *Izaak Walton's "The Compleat Angler"*; and David Hill Radcliffe, "'Study to be Quiet': Genre and Politics in Izaak Walton's 'The Compleat Angler,'" *ELR* 22 (Winter 1992): 95-111.

champions memory as a way of preserving the identity of the Anglican community and their values in the midst of the oppression experienced in the Civil War.

In the *Compleat Angler*, Izaak Walton incorporates a wide range of earlier piscatory poetry and lore—as well as a variety of other forms—to construct a "commonplace book" of fishing poems, songs, and instruction. The piscatory content is conveyed through a dialogue between Piscator, who is the angler (and angling teacher) and Viator—the "wayfarer" (and student). Not only do the two talk and fish; they also walk together from Tottenham toward Ware, and then back along the road toward London. In the course of their journey, they stop at inns and alehouses, and encounter pastoral characters such as shepherds and milkmaids. The external action of Walton's book is at its simplest level a narrative of pastoral withdrawal from and return to the city. But as critics of the *Compleat Angler* have long observed, Walton's book is far more complex than this simple outline conveys. For through his dialogic structure, Walton creates a pastoral community that coheres through an emphasis on envisioning and remembering both fishing instruction and shared values.

Walton is not original in linking angling with remembering. Indeed, angling was a common metaphor in the Middle Ages for culling knowledge from books and imprinting those various pieces of knowledge in an orderly fashion in the memory—and then for recalling that information from the mind.[3] Furthermore, in fifteenth- and sixteenth-century English fishing treatises, "angling" emerges as a metaphor for gathering knowledge about, and writing

---

[3] For example, Quintilian asserts that "as even the various kinds of fish flourish in different surroundings . . . so not every kind of argument [comes from just any place]." Or again, Geoffrey of Vinsauf encourages his students to "practice the contents of their memorial store, laid away with markers of whatever sorts of *notae* [also called hooks (*unci*)] suit them. Otherwise, they will be like a cat, which wants the fish but not the fishing" (cited in Mary Carruthers, *The Book of Memory: A Study of Memory in Medieval Culture* [Cambridge: Cambridge Univ. Press, 1990], p. 62). According to Carruthers, the phrase "Cattus amat piscus, sed non vult tangere flumen," "A cat loves fish, but does not want to touch the river," is proverbial (see W. W. Skeat, Early English Proverbs) (quoted in Mary Carruthers, *The Book of Memory*, p. 345, n. 66).

and reading about, the activity itself of angling.[4] In his book, Walton foregrounds, through fishing metaphor, this mnemonic element. His anglers not only "catch" fish; they also mentally angle the history of, songs about, and instruction and knowledge of, fishing. Through the dialogue, the characters create verbal "images"—word pictures—through their description and instruction of fish and angling. By imprinting these images and facts in their minds, the characters "remember" both the values of the community to which they belong, and the spiritual tenets that they are exhorted as a group to uphold.

The visual elements of the *Compleat Angler* serve a function similar to that of Renaissance emblem books which are meant, according to Huston Diehl, to "stimulate the reader to recollect spiritual truths, to remember what is not present or visible."[5] As William Engels contends, "Renaissance metaphorics was essentially mnemonic and emblematic"; emblem and memory lie at the core of Renaissance culture.[6] The engravings, dialogue, and word pictures of Walton serve the function of what Engels calls the "monitory" memory: memory that draws on the past, "reminds" of the future, and instructs about the present (57). Cicero had made "memory" a subset of Prudence, and thereby of Virtue;[7] and the ability of memory to help the individual live a virtuous life was emphasized throughout the Middle Ages, and into the Renaissance.[8] Indeed, the *Compleat Angler* can be seen as the representation of a kind of "emblem book" or "memory house" constructed by Walton, a collection of images pointing from physical representations of fish

---

[4] See especially Breton, *Wits Trenchmour: In a Conference Had, Betwixt a Scholler and an Angler* (1597). See also Juliana Bernes, *Treatyse of Fysshynge wyth an Angle* (1496), and John Dennys, *The Secrets of Angling* (1613).

[5] Huston Diehl, "Graven Images: Protestant Emblem Books in England," *Renaissance Quarterly* 39 (1986): 57.

[6] William E. Engel, *Mapping Mortality: The Persistence of Memory and Melancholy in Early Modern England* (Amherst: Univ. of Massachusetts Press, 1995), 3; hereafter cited in text.

[7] Cicero, *De inventione. De optimo genere oratorum*, tr. H. M. Hubbell (Cambridge, Mass: Harvard Univ. Press, 1949), 2.53.160.

[8] See Frances Yates, *The Art of Memory* (Chicago: Univ. of Chicago Press, 1966), 73-4, on Aquinas's notion of memory and virtue.

and the art of angling, to a celebration of Anglican cultural values and of unseen spiritual "truths."

Walton provides actual engravings on both the title page and throughout the work which are, as Jonquil Bevan asserts, exceptionally done.[9] In his "To the Reader," Walton says that "he that likes not the discourse, should like the pictures of the Trout and other fish."[10] The title page engraving is a sort of emblem, a cartouche comprised of angry sea fish, waves and curves (the volatile "seas" of William Basse's poem,[11] and the dangerous world of the sea sermons[12]), itself framed by the straight, simple lines of both fishing lines and caught fresh-water fish (prizes of the simple, ordered life). Within the treatise, Walton provides physical "pictures" of various types of fish, pictures that the reader is invited to contemplate as he or she reads the dialogue.

The *Compleat Angler* is obsessed with space and the visual, with hiding and revealing both objects and information, with secrets and the disclosure of knowledge. The words of the dialogue constantly point out their inability fully to disclose adequate

---

[9] Bevan, *Izaak Walton's "The Compleat Angler,"* 40-3. The 1653 edition includes engravings of the trout, pike carp, tench, perch, and barbell.

[10] Izaak Walton, *The Compleat Angler* (1653), ed. Jonquil Bevan (Oxford: Clarendon Press, 1983), 59; all quotations from *The Compleat Angler* will be taken from this edition and cited in text as *CA*.

[11] "I care not, I, to fish in seas, / Fresh rivers best my mind do please" (*CA* 96).

[12] See, for example, John Donne: "The world is a Sea . . . as it is subject to stormes, and tempests . . . as it is bottomlesse to any line . . . as it hath ebbs and floods, and no man knowes the true reason of those floods and those ebbs" (John Donne, Sermons 13-4, "Mat.18-20: And Jesus . . . saith unto them, Follow me, and I will make you Fishers of Men," Preached at the Haghe Dec. 19, 1619; revised in 1630. In *The Sermons of John Donne*, ed. George Potter and Evelyn Simpson [Berkeley, Univ. of California Press, 1955], 2:306. See also Samuel Hieron, *The Spiritual Fishing* (London, 1618): "Thus wee see how the World is compared to the Sea. The state of the Sea is uncertaine, so is the World; it is tempestuous, so is the World full of tumult; In it the great fishes devour the lesse; so in the World the poore and weake are a spoile to the mighty: Leviathan takes his pleasures in the Sea, so doth Satan rule and bear sway in the world."

knowledge and information. Walton acknowledges from the beginning that:

> how to make a man that was none, an Angler by a book: he that undertakes it, shall undertake a harder task then *Hales*, that in his printed Book undertook by it to teach the Art of Fencing, and was laught at for his labour. . . . [T]hat Art was not to be taught by words, nor is the Art of Angling. (*CA* 60)

And Piscator repeatedly asserts to Viator that words, or discourse, are not adequate to teach one to angle; that "observation and practice" must supplement language (*CA* 107). In the *Compleat Angler*, observation and emulation, in addition to appropriate attention to discourse, are essential to learning both how to fish, and how to live a virtuous life.

Piscator repeatedly points out to Viator information or knowledge that words cannot convey. For example, regarding the use of minnow for bait, Piscator asserts: "I cannot well teach in *words*, but must *shew* you how to put it on your hook, that it may turn the better" (*CA* 103; my emphasis in quotations throughout this paragraph). Or again, regarding fishing with live bait, "*experience* will teach you better then I can by *words*" (*CA* 125). Later, concerning the "Roch and Dace," Piscator asserts that Viator may "bear any common Angler *company* that fishes for them, and by that means learn more then any direction I can give you in *words*, can make you capable of; and I will therefore end my *discourse*" (*CA* 147). Toward the end, Piscator says of all of the discourse:

> These, my honest scholer, are some observations told to you as they now come suddenly into my memory, of which you may make some use: but for the practical part, it is that that makes an Angler; it is *diligence*, and *observation*, and *practice* that must do it. (*CA* 157)[13]

---

[13] These are just a few of the many instances of such assertions by Piscator. See also: "I must take time to tel it you hereafter; or indeed, you must learn it by observation and practice" (*CA* 87); "there is your Rod and line; and my advice is, that you fish as you see mee do, and try which can catch the first fish" (*CA* 106); "to see a fly made by another, is the best

Talk—even virtuous discourse—cannot make an angler, or a virtuous man.

David Radcliffe points out elements of Walton's discourse that he sees as especially suited to an Anglican writing during the Interregnum, elements that counter the plethora of contentious arguments circulated at the time: "clear and distinct arguments were met with opposing arguments equally clear and distinct."[14] The discourse of Walton's treatise indeed stands in stark contrast to such argumentative works. To compensate for the limits of language, Walton sometimes simply lets the discourse point beyond itself to that which must be observed (and which requires community, a shared activity). Elsewhere, he supplements the discourse with engravings of fish, or with song. And often, he uses words to paint pictures of figures worthy of emulation or contemplation. In his emphasis on the visual, Walton counters the militant Protestant privileging of hearing (the word) over sight. In the *Compleat Angler*, words are necessary tools for creating images, or for revealing to the reader those images in Walton's memory. These words are set in a dialogic (narrative and geographical) framework, and are conveyed not as ends in themselves, but to refer beyond themselves to the images they convey. These images, then, are to be taken up into the individual (and communal) memory.

As Piscator transmits the content of his memory to Viator throughout the dialogue, Viator explicitly builds with it a "house" in his memory as he stores the instructions, as well as songs he hears, in spaces in his mind. On the return trip to London, Viator

---

teaching to make it, and then an ingenuous Angler may walk by the River and *mark* what fly falls on the water that day" (*CA* 109); "the rest must be taught you by practice, for time will not alow me to say more" (*CA* 127); "And for your dead bait for a *Pike*, for that you may be taught by one dayes going a fishing with me or any other body that fishes for him, for the baiting your hook with a dead *Gudgion* or a *Roch*, and moving it up and down the water, is too easie a thing to take up any time to direct you to do it" (*CA* 127).

[14] Radcliffe, "Study to be Quiet," 103, 97. See also James Holstun, ed., *Pamphlet Wars: Prose in the English Revolution* (Portland, Oreg.: Frank Cass, 1992), for essays on some of the popular prose pamphlets written at the time.

urges Piscator to "be still so courteous as to give me more instructions, for I have several boxes in my memory in which I will keep them all very safe, and there shall not one of them be lost" (*CA* 152). And upon hearing the last verses recited by Piscator, Viator asserts that "these be Verses that be worthy to keep a room in every mans memory. I thank you for them, and I thank you for your many instructions, which I will not forget" (*CA* 163). Piscator is impressed by the "good" and "happie memorie" of Viator, who is able to recall within the dialogue verses he has learned in the past (*CA* 137-8). Viator speaks of his memory in spatial terms, as do classical and many Renaissance rhetoricians. Walton shows Viator either storing or retrieving "images" on or from his "place" of memory.

Walton works within the classical "art of memory," whereby "images" are imprinted on "loci" in the mind. According to the "architectural mnemonic," a classical mnemonic whose use continued through the Middle Ages and well into the seventeenth century, the individual first constructs an architectural structure in his mind (a palace, a house, a room), and then impresses various "images" in a particular order in that "locus," such that they can be retrieved in any order on demand.[15] According to the author of *Ad Herennium* (c.86-82 B.C.), who spells this mnemonic out most fully, loci are "such scenes as are naturally or artificially set off . . . for example, a house" (209).[16] And he recommends choosing loci rather "in a deserted than in a populous region, because the crowding and passing to and fro of people confuse and weaken the impress of the images" (211). The image, "a figure, mark, or portrait of the object we wish to remember" (209), should be "strong and sharp and suitable for awakening recollection" (219), and placed in an ordered fashion in a locus.

This classical art of memory continued to be explored and practiced even in the mid-seventeenth century,[17] and Walton builds

---

[15] See Mary Carruthers, "The Architectural Mnemonic," in *The Book of Memory*, 71-9. See also Yates, *The Art of Memory*.

[16] *Herennium de ratione dicendi (Rhetorica ad Herennium)*, tr. Harry Caplan (Cambridge: Harvard Univ. Press, 1954), III.xvi-xxiv; hereafter cited in text by page.

[17] For example, Francis Bacon, a chief source of Walton, defines memory as consisting of "place of memory" and "emblem," which

on this art in his angling book. In the *Compleat Angler*, the notion of "place," of "locus," the tracing of a geography, is an important feature, for Walton depicts actual landmarks in the English countryside. The fishing advice, songs, and lore become associated in the *Compleat Angler* with specific geographical or architectural features—and these associations aid both Viator (the learner) and the reader of Walton's book in their ability to remember what is being conveyed. Piscator and Viator meet near Tottenham and walk together "along the road which follows the Lea valley from Tottenham to Ware";[18] and after two days' retreat, return along the road toward London. Along the way, Viator and Piscator mention, describe, or visit various inns: the Thatcht house ("a real inn at Hoddesdon" [*CA* 375]); Trout Hall (where they apparently never go [*CA* 83]); and Bleak-Hall (*CA* 84, 89). Bleak-Hall is described as

> an honest Alehouse, where we shall find a cleanly room, Lavender in the windowes, and twenty Ballads stuck about the wall; there my Hostis (which I may tel you, is both cleanly and conveniently handsome) has drest many a one [fish] for me. (*CA* 83)

Like images in a memory house, the ballads are "stuck about the wall" of the inn;[19] and many of the songs sung by the characters in the dialogue are likewise "remembered" under the roofs of the inns. Furthermore, Piscator and Viator exchange information at different

---

"reduceth conceits intellectual to images sensible, which strike the memory more" (Francis Bacon, *The Advancement of Learning* XV.3, cited from *The Advancement of Learning and New Atlantis*, ed. Arthur Johnston [Oxford: Clarendon Press, 1974], 130). John Willis's *Art of Memory* (1621), was reprinted in 1661 as *Mnemonica; or, the Art of Memory, Drained out of the pure Fountains of Art & Nature. Digested into Three Books. Also, A Physical Treatise of cherishing Natural Memory; diligently collected out of divers learned mens Writing* (London, 1661).

[18] Bevan, notes to the *Compleat Angler*, 375.

[19] Cf. Donne's definition of memory as "the Gallery of the soul . . . hang'd with so many, and so lively pictures of the goodness and mercies of thy God to thee, as that everyone of them shall be a catechism to thee" (*Sermons of John Donne*, vol 2, p.237 [Sermon 11]).

points along the way. For example, on the road toward Ware, Piscator relates the antiquity and commendation of the art (ch. 1); they "walk a mile" from the place of hunting otters to that of catching chub, during which time they discuss inappropriate forms of discourse (*CA* 82); they approach "yonder tree" to catch a chub (*CA* 83); on a walk from Bleak house to the river they discuss the trout (*CA* 98); under a "sycamore tree" they discuss the making of flies (*CA* 106-7), and so forth. The information exchanged, and the songs sung, are imprinted on the pastoral landscape. As *Ad Herennium* would have it, the location is quiet and remote, but a pastoral retreat rather than a building. Walton provides a visual "locus" on which to imprint angling "images." As a result, Viator— like the reader—is better able to absorb and remember the instruction.

The remembering of these images—and the exchange of memories—leads to a sense of shared community. In discussing the antiquity of angling, Piscator gives a number of opinions regarding its origin. Among them are the notions:

> that Seth, one of the Sons of Adam, taught it to his sons, and that by them it was derived to Posterity. Others say, that he left it engraven on those Pillars which hee erected to preserve the knowledg of the Mathematicks, Musick, and the rest of those precious Arts, which by Gods appointment or allowance, and his noble industry were thereby preserved from perishing in Noah's Floud. (*CA* 68)

The first account suggests the passing down of angling information through verbal exchanges, exchanges similar to those between Piscator and Viator, and emphasizes the importance of history, community, and shared knowledge. But the latter account intensifies all of those emphases, for it brings the instruction into the realm of image, which is crucial for remembering. Like a memory image, or the woodcuts in Walton's text, the art is pictorially represented such that it outlives even catastrophic events:

floods, even wars.[20] The account mirrors Walton's undertaking in the *Compleat Angler.* Piscator passes the art down to Viator, his scholar; and that knowledge is "engraven" in images and stored in memory loci in Viator's mind. As angling is preserved visually on an architectural structure, so Walton presents the image of two men walking through the geography he creates, talking about and demonstrating aspects of angling—an activity, an image, that points beyond itself to (that aids in the memory of) remembering the values of the Anglican community through living a virtuous and ordered life. And the "images" of the anglers on the "locus" of the journey from and to London are meant to be imprinted on the mind of the reader, as well.

The instructions that Viator is shown "storing" in the "boxes" in his memory are transmitted specifically and directly from the "memory" of Piscator. In the beginning, Piscator speaks of his instructions as disclosure: "my resolution is to hide nothing from him [Viator]" (*CA* 93). But as the men's intimacy grows, as Viator increasingly demonstrates himself to be fit for the brotherhood, Piscator speaks in terms of transmitting all of his memory to Viator: "I will promise you that as you and I fish, and walk to morrow towards London [the return trip], if I have now forgotten any thing, that I can then *remember,* I will not keep it from you" (*CA* 147). Or again, "I will hide nothing from you that I can *remember*" (*CA* 152); "These . . . are some observations told to you as they come suddenly into my *memory*" (*CA* 157).[21] If images of Viator's memory are of storage and hiding, those of Piscator are of revelation and disclosure: the oral transmission of his memory to Viator.

In the *Compleat Angler,* the notions of memory, secret, and tradition appear repeatedly in relation to one another. It seems natural that as an Anglican writing during the interregnum, Walton would emphasize "tradition," that which was passed down through the church, and was being suppressed by Puritans in those years. Furthermore, "tradition" is distinct from the written word; it

---

[20] Cf. Dennys, *The Secrets of Angling,* in which he argues that Deucalion and Pyrra invented angling as a means of sustaining the newly animated human population after the Deucalion flood.

[21] See also Piscator's assertion: "I will tell you, as they shall come into my mind, more observations" (*CA* 109).

consists of knowledge, songs, ideas passed down by word of mouth, from generation to generation. And that tradition is preserved in the "memory," which may look back nostalgically on the past (before the Civil War), and which, as we have seen above, ideally takes the form of images imprinted on places. Frequently in the *Compleat Angler*, the knowledge passed down to the memory through tradition takes the form of "secrets" stored in the minds of a limited few. A member of the "Brotherhood of the Angle" (there were a number of closed guilds and secret societies in the seventeenth century),[22] Piscator would be expected to have secret knowledge of his trade. This secret knowledge becomes the most desired, even as it is the most hidden, information in the treatise.

Piscator speaks frequently about the breeding, storage, and use of live baits (worms, flies, etc.), which are generally kept in closed containers. These containers become in the course of the *Compleat Angler* metaphors for memory boxes in individuals' minds, particularly those "boxes" that store secrets. For example, Piscator tells Viator a "secret" about a fellow angler, Oliver Henly, who "would usually take three or four worms out of his bag and put them into a little box in his pocket, where he would usually let them continue half an hour or more, before he would bait his hook with them" (120). In order to keep his secret, Henly misleads the other anglers about the technique—a technique that involves anointing the worms in an oil that gives them a scent particularly attractive to the fish. One of Henly's "most intimate and secret friends," however, has disclosed the secret of the "little box" to Piscator. The storage of the secret ointment in a literal box mirrors the storage of that secret in the memory boxes of Henly's mind. The entire passage is a "reminiscence" of Piscator (or Walton), a memory of a series of past events that had not been recorded in writing. Furthermore, the episode demonstrates the communal transmission of memory: Henly passes the secret to a "secret friend," who passes it to Piscator, who passes it on to Viator.

---

[22] For discussions of these groups, see Stella Kramer, *The English Craft Gilds: Studies in their Progress and Decline* (New York: Columbia Univ. Press, 1927); R. A. Leeson, *Travelling Brothers: The Six Centuries' Road from Craft Fellowship to Trade Unionism* (London: George Allen, 1979), pt. 1; and Timothy Raylor, *Cavaliers, Clubs, and Literary Culture* (Newark, N.J.: Univ. of Delaware Press, 1994).

In a similar passage, Piscator conveys to Viator one of his memories about another oil for catching fish, and another inaccessible secret:

> There be several Oiles of a strong smel that I have been told of, and to be excellent to tempt fish to bite, of which I could say much, I remember I once carried a small bottle from Sir George Hastings to Sir Henry Wotton . . . as a great present; but upon enquiry, I found it did not answer the expectation of Sir Henry, which with the help of other circumstances, makes me have little belief in such things . . . but there is a mysterious knack [to anointing baits], which . . . lies locked up in the braine or brest of some chimical men, that . . . yet will not reveal it. (*CA* 154)

The passage is comprised of a series of enclosures within enclosures: the entire incident is recounted from within the "memory" of Piscator ("I remember"); the secret oil is in "a small bottle," an enclosed container. The knowledge of this type of ointment is, itself, "locked up in the braine or brest of some chimical men," undisclosed even to other members of the community or brotherhood. Piscator speaks with a certain removed irony here: he has "little belief in such things," and the oil had disappointed Wotton. But Piscator's interest in stored information which might be usefully conveyed to the community remains a consistent concern in his discourse.

These examples—Henly's storage of a secret in boxes and in his mind, the knowledge "locked up in the braine or brest of some chimical men"—are images of hiding away, of closing off from sight, even from the sight of other anglers. That which is hidden (like the fish to be caught) is strongly desired: several men are curious about and determined to investigate and discuss the secret in Henly's "little box," and Piscator is desirous of the inaccessible "mysterious knack" of anointing baits. These are secrets stored in the memories of individuals, unwritten and therefore, if not conveyed through discourse, lost to posterity. Some secrets, it seems, are kept hidden even from the community.

Elsewhere in the discourse, Walton links "secrets" specifically to the oral tradition of a particular group. In so doing, Walton images forth the use of secrets not just for personal gain, but also for the health of the community. Piscator articulates one particularly potent image of a tradition about the healing power of tenches:

> Randelitius . . . saw certaine Jewes apply Tenches to the feet of a sick man for a cure; and it is observed, that many of those people have many Secrets unknown to Christians, secrets which have never been written, but have been successively since the dayes of Solomon . . . delivered by tradition from the father to the son, and so from generation to generation without writing, or . . . without the least communicating them to any other Nation or Tribe (for to do so, they account a profanation). (*CA* 135)

In this passage, Piscator expands the storage of secret memories beyond the labor of an individual (for example, Henly or the "chimical man") and into that of a community. This community is envisioned by Piscator as passing knowledge down through speech and hearing, "from the father to the son," without writing. To avoid "profanation," to maintain sacredness, the group keeps the knowledge locked in its communal memory. And in this case, that knowledge is a healing power, wisdom that serves to strengthen the health of the group.

The communal aspect of "memory" appears strikingly in the song contests in the *Compleat Angler*, in which the participants are generally praised first not because of their choice of song, or their rendition, but because of their ability to "remember." The characters sing songs of a sort that the Puritans attempted to suppress during these years, and thus the element of the individual contributing to the communal memory is apt. Piscator is "glad my *memory* did not lose these last Verses [of Dennys]," with which he supplements his discourse (*CA* 79; my emphases in quotations throughout this paragraph). He praises the song of Viator, which was "well *remembred* and sung by you" (*CA* 113)—and Piscator encourages him to "*forget not* the Ketch which you promised to make against night" (*CA* 113). Later, Piscator praises Viator again in his singing of Donne's "The Baite": "Well *remembered*, honest Scholer, I thank you for these choice Verses, which I have heard formerly, but had quite forgot, till they were recovered by your happy *memorie*" (*CA* 138). The milkwoman praises her daughter in the same way: "Maudlin . . . hath good *store* of them [ballads]: Maudlin hath a notable *memory*" (*CA* 145). Piscator sings a song, but "having *forgotten* a part of it, I was forced to patch it up by the help of my invention" (*CA* 150). And of the last song, Viator asserts that "these be Verses that be worthy to keep a room in every mans *memory*" (*CA* 163). As Viator stores images in the "boxes" of his memory, so the various characters have "stored" these ballads in their minds, presumably through artificial memory devices (note the spatial imagery: "recovered," "store," "patch it up," "room").

It seems ironic that many of the songs "remembered" in the *Compleat Angler* had been written over half a century before, could have been recovered only through the printed word, and in Walton's book are reprinted in writing. But in portraying the community as "remembering" songs rather than "reading" them, Walton creates a certain kind of community, one that has consciously committed the past, and particularly past standards of conduct and discursive manners, to memory. In depicting a community with good "memories," Walton also provides an example for his reader, whose memory he attempts to stimulate through his discourse.

In his "To the Reader," Walton says of the *Compleat Angler* that it is a "kind of picture of my owne disposition" (*CA* 59). In this description by Walton, the entire book is a "picture," an "emblem" that is inextricably linked with the notion of memory—the memory of Walton, of the community he creates, and ultimately of the reader. "Disposition" here carries a number of meanings beyond "natural tendency or bent of mind."[23] That Walton may paint a "picture" of it suggests that he conceives of it in physical, spatial terms—as something of which an image may be made. Disposition refers to "setting in order . . . relative position of the parts or elements of a whole" (1.a). In rhetoric, the disposition is the "due arrangement of the parts of an argument or discussion" (1.b). Walton plays on these various meanings in his dialogue: the *Compleat Angler* represents Walton's peaceable "frame of mind,"

---

[23] *OED,* "Disposition," 6; hereafter cited in text by number of definition.

and it presents an ordering of information about angling conveyed through the "speech" of Piscator and others.

But "disposition" was also a technical architectural term in the seventeenth century for "the due arrangement of the several parts of a building" (1.c)—and this architectural component is significant to Walton's mnemonic undertaking.[24] Walton presents his work as a picture of his own memory house—an image of the architectural arrangement of his mind. The reader is to take the treatise as "picture," to imprint the locus of geography between London and Ware, and the images of anglers, with their images of fish and other anglers and secrets and baits, onto his or her own memory. These images the reader is to use, as Piscator and Viator use their own images, for purposes of contemplation. At the same time, as Piscator does with Viator, the reader is to transmit to others those images and memories he or she has gained. Walton emphasizes individual and solitary contemplation based on visual images in the memory; but he also emphasizes throughout the importance of transmitting those images to others.

Indeed, toward the end of the *Compleat Angler*, Viator demonstrates his transformation into a member of the "brotherhood of the Angle." He recounts to Piscator, Peter, and Coridon his contemplation when he had been left alone by Piscator. Sitting alone "under a Willow tree by the water side," on the meadow of a rich man who faced pending "Law Suites," Viator had contemplated his surroundings. Viator's contemplation illustrates a specific moment in which sight stimulates virtuous memory:

---

[24] Walton's friend Henry Wotton (who is mentioned in the *Compleat Angler*) had written a treatise on architecture, in which he describes the "Disposition" as a subset (along with "Preparations of the *Materials*") of the "principall parts" (as opposed to the "*Ornaments*") of the "Worke." According to Wotton, the Disposition is the "Forme"; and his discussion of this element (which comprises most of the book) covers the entire structure of the building, from walls to columns to chimneys. In the section on "ornaments," he discusses what would be analogous to "images" in memory—the pictures hung on the wall, sculptures, and so forth. Henry Wotton, *The Elements of Architecture: A Facsimile Reprint of the First Edition (London, 1624)*, introduction and notes by Frederick Hard (Charlottesville: Univ. Press of Virginia, 1968), 10.

> I could there sit quietly, and *looking* on the water, see
> fishes leaping at Flies of several shapes and colours;
> *looking* on the Hils, could behold them spotted with
> Woods and Groves; *looking* down the Meadows, could
> see here a Boy gathering Lillies and Lady-smocks. . . .
> As I thus sate joying in mine own happy condition . . . I
> did thankfully *remember* what my Savior said, that the
> meek possess the earth. (*CA* 150; my emphases)

Viator observes the water, the fishes and colorful flies, the varied
landscape, just as Piscator had taught him. He sits on the land of a
rich but unhappy man who "had a plentiful estate, but not a heart
to think so," and observes a young boy innocently gathering
flowers. As Viator, free from the burdens of the landowner, "looks"
on these things, the images cause him to "remember" a scriptural
"truth." For Viator, the memory quickens the image into
contemplation, an experience that Viator then recounts to those
around him. In this recounting, Viator contributes to the
communal memory store, thereby adding to and perpetuating the
values of the "Brotherhood of the Angle"—and, by extension, of
the Anglican community—the community for whom Walton
writes, and remembers.

Webster University

Marvell and the Temporality of Paranoia

HEATHER HIRSCHFELD

A BOUT 30 years ago, Joan Hartwig delivered a talk at this very conference (it was in Chapel Hill, though, not Raleigh) on "Double Time in Marvell's 'Bermudas'"; it was published in *Renaissance Papers 1974*. Her central argument, an effort to mediate between the competing allegorical and historical interpretations of Rosalie Colie and Emile Legouis, suggested that the poem was capable of presenting "the mutable and non-mutable worlds [as] simultaneously understood." In other words, she explained, although the initial lines of the poem—what we might consider the opening "frame"—are highly indeterminate, setting a boat adrift in no identifiable direction, the poem's interior song or hymn "realizes in precise and sensuous detail" the "things held back from specification in the first four lines." She concluded her reading by suggesting the effect of such a vision, an effect that she seemed to view as satisfyingly, even comfortingly, determined. For the poem, she explained, grants us (and, I assume, its oarsmen) "an experience of paradise and salvation through election, [even as] we are still in progress towards that experience."[1]

Hartwig's analysis depends upon a hermeneutic program that is also implicit in the poem, the program of typological reading. And insofar as her discussion embraces this approach, I am skeptical of her conclusions about the comfort afforded by an experience still in progress. Typology, as Julia Lupton defines it, "describes the exegetical relation between the Old Testament and the New, in which the prior text forms both the hallowed origin and the superseded

---

[1] Joan Hartwig, "Double Time in Marvell's 'Bermudas'" *Renaissance Papers 1974* (Southeastern Renaissance Conference, 1975), 58, 53.

beginnings of the latter work."[2] Its procedures for interpreting were extended in the early modern period to explain contemporary events either as the realization of earlier models or in light of their future fulfillment in later ones. This interpretive endeavor was pursued not only by theologians but by popular writers as well (Thomas Middleton, better known for his acerbic city comedies, arranged related passages on verso and recto leafs in *The Mariage of the Old and New Testaments*, for instance), although this very rigor, demonstrated in a tome like the Oxford divine Thomas Jackson's *The Knowledge of Christ Jesus. The Seventh Book of Commentaries upon the Apostles Creed*, may testify equally to the frailty or tenuousness of the typological enterprise. Indeed, as critics like Debora Shuger or Joseph Wittreich have shown, its procedures were already being interrogated in the Renaissance; writers such as Hooker and Milton treated analogical and anagogical reading as oppressively ahistorical or unequivocal.[3] Marvell's poetry, I want to suggest in this paper, can be seen as similarly suspicious of such an interpretive program, but his suspicion takes a different form than these others. In the readings that follow, I show that Marvell's poems give voice to a critique of typology as a hermeneutic system that, even as it proposes to help interpreters come to terms with originary and subsequent losses, only resituates them in overdetermined structures of defeat from which they cannot escape and for which they can find neither adequate cause nor sustainable recompense. The promises and failings of this kind of reading, I conclude, can be construed as "paranoid." Hartwig's "double time" is in Marvell the temporality of paranoia.

When applied to Renaissance literature, the term paranoia is usually reserved to describe dramatic characters. Critical accounts of

---

[2] Julia Lupton, *Afterlives of the Saints: Hagiography, Typology and Renaissance Literature* (Stanford: Stanford Univ. Press, 1996), xvii.

[3] Debora Shuger, *Habits of Thought in the English Renaissance* (Toronto: Toronto Univ. Press, 1990), 30-5; Joseph Wittreich, *Interpreting "Samson Agonistes"* (Princeton: Princeton Univ. Press), 180-1. But see Thomas Hester, "Typology and Parody in 'Upon the Circumcision,'" for a discussion of how typology can be both universalizing and historicizing: "The typology of the Circumcision, thus, provides a sign (a 'seal') of divine meaning amidst historical contexts" (*Renaissance Papers 1985* [Southeastern Renaissance Conference, 1986], 67).

Leontes and Othello, for instance, have explained their sexual jeal-
ousies as the result of epistemological crises that jeopardize their
ability to know and trust others, sending them into a spiral of delusional contempt and rage. Most recently, Linda Charnes has discussed *Hamlet* as "modernity's inaugural paranoid text" and its
eponymous hero as literature's first *noir*—and thus paranoid—
detective. But ideas of paranoia need not be restricted to a theatrical
psyche. If we understand paranoia as Charnes eloquently does, "in
the literal Greek sense as a form of 'overknowing,' of surplus
knowledge that leads, paradoxically, not to discovery but to undecidability,"[4] we can begin to see how a poetic or narrative form,
when guided or inflected by typological paradigms or assumptions,
may function as a paranoid system. For typology both structures
and invites a method of reading that assumes "too much" knowledge: it assumes the knowledge of past events in the future and the
knowledge of future events in the past. Typology is thus a special
kind of "overdetermined" interpretation the result of which, as
Charnes suggests, is, ironically, uncertainty. Robert Burton describes this uncertainty of "overknowing" in *The Anatomy of Melancholy* as a cause of psychic incapacitation. He chides those who,
"with a deal of foolish presumption, curiosity, needless speculation,
contemplation, solicitude . . . trouble and puzzle themselves about
those questions of grace, free will, perseverance, God's secrets; they
will know more than is revealed of God in His Word, human capacity or ignorance can apprehend, and too importunate inquiry
after that which is revealed; mysteries, ceremonies, observation of
Sabbaths, laws, duties, etc."[5] Burton thus sees the perils of too
much knowledge when knowledge is tied to issues of predestination.[6] Marvell's lyrics, I argue below, present the perils of too much
knowledge when knowledge is tied to a typological hermeneutic.
That is, I suggest that Marvell offers poetic speakers who operate

---

[4] Linda Charnes, "Dismember Me: Shakespeare, Paranoia, and the
Logic of Mass Culture," *Shakespeare Quarterly* (1997): 4.

[5] Robert Burton, *The Anatomy of Melancholy*, ed. Holbrook Jackson
(New York: New York Review of Books, 2001), Part 3, 399.

[6] For a rich treatment of the psychological and sociological effects of
theologies of predestination, see John Stachniewski, *The Persecutory
Imagination: English Puritanism and the Literature of Religious Despair*
(Oxford: Clarendon Press, 1991).

according to a typological excess of knowledge, and that this results in an undecidability that involves various kinds of deprivation or suffering.

This uncertainty is wonderfully apparent in "Bermudas." For the poem's frame denies the achievements proclaimed in its central song of praise. The first lines set a dramatic scene: "Where the remote Bermudas ride / In the ocean's bosom unespied, / From a small boat that rowed along, / The listening winds received this song."[7] The poem then launches into a hymn: "'What shall we do but sing his praise / That led us through the watery maze / Unto an isle so long unknown, / And yet far kinder than our own" (5-8) and it proceeds to catalogue the manifold favors shown unto these pilgrims by a God who "lands us on a grassy stage, / Safe from the storms, and prelates rage. / He gave us this eternal spring / Which here enamels everything" (11-4). Furthermore God "cast[s] (of which we rather boast) / The gospel's pearl upon our coast, / And in these rocks for us did frame / A temple, where to sound his name" (29-32). The hymn—which is itself the genre of thanks for deeds already done—presents the hand of God as having already been shown to the inhabitants of the boat; its tense is present and past, the tense of things already seen and done. But the final four lines snatch away the accomplishment: "Thus sung they, in the English boat, / A holy and a cheerful note, / And all the way, to guide their chime, / With falling oars they kept the time" (37-40). The last four lines do not simply make it impossible to tell, as Hartwig says, where the boat is rowing; they make it impossible to tell whether the pastoral and paradisal depiction that has just been so richly delivered in song has actually been realized. The poem, that is, presents as accomplished a scene of Edenic return that, in the final moment, it denies. This denial, a move on the poet's, and not the pilgrims in the boat's part, turns the singers' hymn into a delusion of, rather than a thanks for, Providential intervention and reward. It is this delusional sensibility—the result, I am arguing, of the interpretive pressures enforced by a hermeneutic system that depends on the realization of types—that registers the song of the boat paranoid. It is not the paranoia of persecution—indeed, the

---

[7] Andrew Marvell, "Bermudas," in *Andrew Marvell*, ed. Keith Walker (Oxford: Oxford Univ. Press, 1990), ll. 1-4. All subsequent citations of Marvell's poetry are to this edition.

pilgrims in the boat have faith in a truly beneficent God—but the paranoia of seeing the future as if it were the past or the present. This is a problem not only of time but also of representation. For the internal hymn blurs the linguistic as well as temporal logic of question and reply. "'What should we do but sing his praise'," the boaters ask in the first line after the opening frame, "'That led us through the watery maze'." As the song becomes a chronicle of God's gifts, it turns the query into its own answer, a temporal and representational recursivity that, in a fashion I am calling paranoid, makes interpretation over in the image of its object.

The same recursivity characterizes the end of "The Nymph Complaining," in which the nymph envisions herself as a statue that cries self-inscribing tears. It is one of the most remarkable images in the Marvell canon:

> First my unhappy statue shall
> Be cut in marble; and withal,
> Let it be weeping too—but there
> The engraver sure his art may spare,
> For I so truly thee bemoan,
> That I shall weep though I be stone:
> Until my tears, still dropping, wear
> My breast, themselves engraving there (111-18).

The depiction here of "auto-imprinting," not unlike the hymn that becomes an answer to its own question, is the logical extreme of a hermeneutic that sees one set of events as the necessary fulfillment—or the necessary origin—of other ones. It turns representation into self-inscription. Such a process can be seen, among other ways, as the outcome of what Julia Lupton calls the "foreclosure" of typology, the way it eliminates contingency or possibility in favor of a prescribed, or overdetermined, structure.

The nymph participates in and suffers from such a program over the course of the poem. Its initial horror—the murder of the fawn—is at first understood by the nymph as an accident or mistake, the result of the actions of "wanton troopers riding by." But the nymph cannot sustain such a view, and she demands, "E'en beasts must be with justice slain." Lucy Gent has suggested that in Marvell's work speakers like the nymph make such demands out of a human compulsion to see in events purposive design, a compul-

sion which Marvell more or less gently mocks. For the nymph the
need for teleology or purpose takes a theological shape in the practice of typology, a practice that, while it seems to offer explanation
or comfort, has quite devastating effects. It is not simply that she
envisions the fawn as a type of Christ and the troopers as the soldiers at Calvary—"their stain / Is dyed in such a purple grain, /
There is not such another in / The world, to offer for their sin" (21-
4)—an effort that also turns her into a type of the mourning
Madonna. It is that she is forced to consider the shooting in light
of a prior event—here a prior betrayal by one man, Sylvio: "Uncon-
stant Sylvio, when yet / I had not found him counterfeit . . . Gave it
to me" (25-7). Such thinking does indeed do "double time"; it en-
compasses two memories of Sylvio as well as the present state of the
fawn. But such timing is claustrophobically circumscribed. It requires the nymph to think about Sylvio—whose innocence the
nymph cannot invoke without reference first to its lapse—in a way
that simultaneously imagines the fawn's future treachery. "Had it
lived long, I do not know / Whether it too might have done so / As
Sylvio did" (47-9). Constructing a typological scheme organized
around Sylvio's betrayal thus makes the fawn's death both necessary—the outcome of its inheritance from Sylvio—and secondary—
always after his master.

But even this supposedly second betrayal is revealed, as the
nymph continues her account, to have already happened. For the
exquisite depiction of the fawn amongst the lilies in her garden only
sets up, insists on, his death. The nymph has a "garden of my own,"
as she says, where the fawn, lying in beds of lilies, would disappear
from her view:

> For, in the flaxen lilies' shade,
> It like a bank of lilies laid.
> Upon the roses it would feed,
> Until its lips e'en seemed to bleed:
> . . .
> But all its chief delight was still
> On roses this itself to fill:
> And its pure virgin limbs to fold
> In whitest sheets of lilies cold.
> Had it lived long, it would have been
> Lilies without, roses within. (81-92)

The fawn has become quite literally the garden bed. The nymph's portrayal is the reverse of metaphor, in that the fawn has become the object meant to describe him. Her portrayal, in other words, is, in an extended version of the word, perfectly typological: it predicts a later loss by explaining or imagining an earlier one. The description is thus the obverse of the singers' hymn: whereas they turned the future into the past, the nymph turns the past—Sylvio's departure, the fawn's lily bed—into the future. In so doing it simultaneously ensures and predicts that the fawn realizes—in his death—the model of betrayal inherited from Sylvio. The nymph's pathetic mourning, even in what critics have seen as its narcissistic naivety, is a form of Charnes's overknowing whose result is not so much undecidability but loss. The poetic structure suggests that the fawn was lost to the nymph before it was shot.

This sense of loss and its connection to typology is especially acute in "The Garden." Critics, of course, have noted Marvell's ironic play with the Daphne and Syrinx myths; as Marshall Grossman says, the fourth stanza offers a "typological parody of Ovidian metamorphosis—which is, of course, equally, an Ovidian parody of typology."[8] But the poem does not only parody typology, it also reproduces its terms and effects. This reproduction may be inherent in the pastoral, a genre whose premise—the possibility of reaching or regaining a better place that has already been lost— seems inevitably tied to the fundamentally typological notions of prospect and return. Here, however, Marvell uses this imbrication or commitment to show typology as impossible to sustain to even according to its own vision. In the poem's famous eighth stanza, the speaker says:

> Such was that happy garden-state,
> While man there walked without a mate;
> After a place so pure, and sweet,
> What other help could yet be meet!
> But 'twas beyond a mortal's share
> To wander solitary there:
> Two paradises 'twere in one
> To live in paradise alone. (57-64)

---

[8] Marshall Grossman, *The Story of All Things* (Durham, NC: Duke Univ. Press, 1998), 31.

I add to the wealth of criticism on these lines only the point that, having reached in his retreat the paradisal state that is both the source and goal—the past and the future—of typological yearning, the speaker cannot be satisfied. For as long as his "wondrous life" is interpreted according to a scheme that sees Fall and Redemption always in relation to the other—a scheme that ensures that any thought of a paradise regained always involves the recognition of a paradise lost—the speaker must insist on a return not *to* paradise but *before* it. In so doing, in recognizing the happiest state as solitary, he is forced to confront a loss even before the loss of Eden, the loss of his isolation. The withdrawal of the mind into happiness has doubled his misery rather than escaped or surmounted it. Escape, as the ninth stanza makes clear, requires the annihilation of human consciousness altogether.

The speaker's vision, developed like the nymph's, from typological imperatives, is what I am calling paranoid. To say this is not to diagnose speaker, poem, or even poet in psychiatric terms. Indeed, I do not think, as Charnes does of Hamlet, that the nymph or the speaker of "The Garden" is paranoid. Rather, it is to call attention to the way a hermeneutic—and here a hermeneutic with particular hegemony in the early periods—can be seen to obey or to foster a fundamentally psychotic structure. At its most extreme—and this is the version to which Marvell stretches it—typology calls for a form of interpretation that is always both overdetermined and, at least until the apocalypse, never fully available.

We have seen this structure operating in Marvell's poems at the level of time—for his speakers the past is understood as the future or the future the past—or at the level of representation—questions become answers, subjects become objects. Such operations seem initially to be designed to restore hope in the lost or fallen world with the prospect of a new or better one that has already been fulfilled by the advent of Christ. But as Marvell's poems reveal, typological structures can perform precisely the opposite: they tend to recall, rather than redeem, earlier losses or pains. Thus the nymph weeps for a fawn whose betrayal has already been accomplished, or the speaker of "The Garden" annihilates everything only to discover his loss of paradise is doubled. I am calling this paradigm paranoid not because it keeps returning speakers to an earlier scene of despair but because failure is written into its very promise. This paradigm is the delusion of typology, at least according to Marvell's poetics.

These poetics have functioned in this reading as kind of "test case"; I have used Marvell's lyrics in order to speculate on aspects of the broader interpretive principles his work was heir to. My sense is that we have perhaps too easily and too quickly assumed that typology, one of the normative hermeneutic systems Renaissance thinkers were heir to, always carries a comforting and satisfying message even if it also reminds us that we still have work to do before any promised end will be fulfilled. A psychoanalytic vocabulary—although not, as I mention above, a psychological diagnosis—allows us to see the way in which a paranoiac structure is embedded in a typological hermeneutic: the latter gives rise to an excess of knowledge and, concomitantly, to a lack of certainty, both of which reinforce an undecidability they were meant to transcend. Recognizing this structure may help us better understand the extent to which early modern epistemological and hermeneutical systems could enforce their own, historically specific, forms of psychic panic.

University of Tennessee, Knoxville

Familiar Letters: Donne and Pietro Aretino

Dennis Flynn

O NE of Donne's earliest extant letters apparently responded to a request by Henry Wotton for a copy of Pietro Aretino's translation of the seven penitential psalms. Donne answered by passing judgment on Aretino's writings in general, finding "most good" in his letters:

> I am sory you should (with any great earnestnes) desyre any thing of P Aretinus not that he could infect; but that it seemes you are alredy infected with the common opinion of him: beleeve me he is much lesse than his fame and was too well payd by the Roman church in that coyne which he coveted most where his bookes were by the counsell of Trent forbidden which if they had beene permitted to have beene worne by all long ere this had beene worne out: his divinyty was but a sirrops to enwrapp his prophane bookes to get them passage yet in these bookes which have devine titles there is least harme as in his letters most good his others have no other singularyty in them but that they are forbidden. The psalmes (which you aske) If I cannot shortly pro- cure you one to poses I can and will at any tyme borrow for you.[1]

---

[1] Donne to Henry Wotton, n. d.; Leicestershire Record Office, Finch Collection, D.G.7, Lit. 2 (Burley Manuscript), f. 309; printed in Simpson, *Prose Works of Donne*, 316-7. Aretino's *Gli Sette Salmi di Penitentia di David* was published at Venice in 1536.

Contrasted to the generally disparaging tone of these comments, Donne's reference to Aretino's letters is a possible clue to his early development as a letter writer, one that as far as I know has never been examined. But Donne's interest in Aretino's letters also implies his more general interest, audible in the fineness of distinctions made here (as well as in the comprehensive range of Donne's judgments) about Aretino's other writings.

That of all people Henry Wotton evidently had consulted Donne as a resource (and maybe even an authority on Aretino) is in itself a striking fact. Fluent in Italian, Wotton was considered one of the best read Englishmen of his time, especially in continental literatures. He had lived nearly two years in Italy, and had by then certainly become acquainted with some of Aretino's work. The Italian writer was notorious for his pornography, including the *Ragionamenti della Nanna e della Antonia,* dialogues of an old harlot and her daughter, who converse for six days concerning the sexual practices of nuns, wives, and prostitutes; and also for the *Sonetti Lussuriosi,* twenty-six sonnets describing modes of sexual intercourse. Donne clearly had read these writings, as no doubt had Wotton. Donne alluded to the *Sonetti* in his "Satyre IV" where, replying to a courtier's suggestion that he learn to appreciate the virtues of the royal Court, the satirist sneers, "Aretines pictures have made few chast."[2] (Aretino's sonnets were captions for engravings by Marcantonio Raimondi, based on drawings by Giulio Romano; the poet was proverbially though erroneously given credit for the pictures as well as the sonnets.) Donne's allusions to these sonnets, in "Satyre IV" as well as in *Ignatius His Conclave* some fifteen years later, were conventional, in keeping with the way Elizabethan and Jacobean writers generally referred to Aretino. But it is clear from Donne's early letter to Wotton that, unlike most of these writers, he was also familiar with the rest of Aretino's works, while he found value especially in the *Lettere.*

Just as noteworthy is the fact that Donne thought he could procure for Wotton a copy of Aretino's translations of the penitential psalms, or (failing that) knew where he could borrow one. All Aretino's works were already rare, having forty years earlier been

---

[2] *The Complete Poetry of John Donne,* ed. John T. Shawcross (Garden City, NY: Anchor Books, 1967), 28.

placed on the Index, as Donne says.[3] Publication of his books in
Italy had ceased, and booksellers' entire stocks had been burned.
Nevertheless, Donne claims ready access to Aretino's psalms. At
least three volumes by Aretino were published in England after
1588: reprints in Italian of his well known pornographic dialogues;
a volume of his four comedies (including *La Cortigiana*, a satire on
the life of the courtier); and the satirical dialogue *Ragionamento
delle Corti*, again ridiculing the Court. Although tricked out with
false Italian imprints, editions of all three books were actually produced by the London publisher John Wolfe, who sold a few copies
of them domestically but evidently produced them mainly for ex-
port. Wolfe had also been licensed to print an edition of Aretino's
letters, although no copy of the *Lettere* published by Wolfe is extant.[4] Perhaps significant in this connection is the five-volume edition of Aretino's *Lettere* listed, along with all three of Wolfe's
known editions of Aretino, among books Donne is thought to have
used, in the library of his friend Henry Percy, ninth Earl of North-

---

[3] Donne is imprecise in attributing an Index to the Council of Trent,
which did not issue any such document. Donne is thinking of the Index
issued by Pope Pius V, mandated by the Council of Trent (as an ameliora-
tion of the truly fanatical index of Paul IV!).

[4] Adolf Gerber, "All of the Five Fictitious Italian Editions of Writings
of Machiavelli and Three of Those of Pietro Aretino Printed by John
Wolfe of London (1584-1589)," *Modern Language Notes* 22 (1907): 5.
Wolfe was licensed to print these works of Aretino in September and Oc-
tober 1588. See also Harry Sellers, "Italian Books Printed in England Before 1640," *The Library*, 4th ser., 5 (1924): 110-1: "Some of Aretino's
works were in the Index in 1557, all in 1558, and this was the beginning
of a veritable persecution against them, so effective that his name disappears completely from Italian books of the century, and the suppression
went on increasing. This was Wolfe's chance to print an English edition
of some of them, to which he gave Italian imprints for the same reason as
[Giordano] Bruno's printer, namely to increase their sale, English printing
of Italian having no reputation. Bruno's statement to the Venetian inquisi-
tor is well known: 'All those books of mine, which say in their imprint
that they were printed in Venice, were printed in England, and it was the
printer who would put on them that they were printed in Venice to sell
them more easily.' Wolfe had the same motives."

umberland. Both Donne and the Earl seem to have been especially interested in Wolfe's enterprise.[5]

In any case, in 1597 Donne promised Wotton access to Aretino's translations of the *Sette Salmi*, a book that must have been extremely hard to come by. Recognized by Wotton as a source for Aretino's books and a connoisseur, Donne accordingly implied in his letter to Wotton that he had read all of Aretino's works, not only the pornography but also the devotional writings and the published letters in which he found "most good." However, Donne's letter to Wotton did not explain how he came to be so familiar with Aretino's writings, or what good he had found in them, especially in the *Lettere*. I have suggested elsewhere a likelihood that Donne traveled to Italy in the 1580s, early travels mentioned but misdated by Izaak Walton. According to Walton, during these early travels Donne spent considerable sums on books.[6] Certainly Italy, and especially Venice, would have been the most likely place to lay hands on copies of Aretino's books, though they were rare even in Italy by the 1580s. Donne's introduction to Aretino's writings may have begun during these travels; but such a matter can hardly be resolved within the scope of this essay. Instead, I will explore Donne's interest in Aretino, beginning with some critically recognized features of Donne's letters that have relation to Aretino's letters, and continuing to discuss other points of relation between Donne and Aretino.

Donne's letters are inadequately used if they are regarded simply as background information, without regard to their genre, their audience, and their context. Margaret Maurer argued that Donne's

---

[5] For the list of Northumberland's books, moved to Syon (his house outside London) from his prison quarters in the Tower in 1614, see Edward Barrington De Fonblanque, *Annals of the House of Percy*, 2 vols. (London: Richard Clay, 1887), 2: 626-30. See also G. R. Batho, "The Library of the 'Wizard' Earl: Henry Percy, Ninth Earl of Northumberland (1564-1632)," *The Library* 15 (1960): 246-61. On Donne's use of Northumberland's library, and on his little regarded but quite important friendship with the Earl, see my "Donne's *Ignatius His Conclave* and Other Libels on Sir Robert Cecil," *JDJ* 6 (1987): 163-83.

[6] "Mr. Donnes estate was the greatest part spent in many and chargeable Travels, Books and dear-bought Experience": Izaak Walton, *The Lives of John Donne, Sir Henry Wotton, Richard Hooker, George Herbert and Robert Sanderson* (London: Oxford Univ. Press, 1956), 30.

letters require explication not entirely or even chiefly because their topical references are remote; more importantly, these letters are difficult for the same reason they have always interested readers: because of Donne's peculiar method as a letter writer, "the various ways Donne uses the device of the letter to locate some image of himself within the press of chronicled events."[7] Donne's familiar letters can supply more than superficial information about his day-to-day activities only if they are read as integral wholes and in awareness of their full context.

Primarily the letters carried to their addressees an impression of Donne's personality and particular circumstances. In one of several informative characterizations of his own letters, Donne told a correspondent that

> I send not my Letters as tribute, nor interest, not recompense, nor for commerce, nor as testimonials of my love, nor provokers of yours, nor to justifie my custome of writing, nor for a vent and utterance of my meditations; for my Letters are either above or under all such offices; yet I write very affectionately, and I chide and accuse my self of diminishing that affection which sends them, when I ask my self why: onely I am sure that I desire that you might have in your hands Letters of mine of all kindes, as conveyances and deliverers of me to you, whether you accept me as a friend, or as a patient, or as a penitent, or as a beadsman, for I decline no jurisdiction, or refuse any tenure. I would not open any doore upon you, but look in when you open it.[8]

Maurer, commenting on this passage, remarked Donne's "particular genius as a letter-writer" in the way he can unite himself with a reader by his choice of detail and his formulation of a relationship. Donne conceives each letter with "a design that has, as its control-

---

[7] "The Poetical Familiarity of John Donne's Letters," *Genre* 15 (1982): 188 and 200.

[8] Donne to Sir Henry Goodyer, n.d.; *Letters to Severall Persons of Honour (1651)*, ed. M. Thomas Hester (Delmar, NY: Scholars' Facsimiles and Reprints, 1977), 109.

ling element, some image of the writer. The result is a self-consistency that makes the letter a world to itself."[9]

John Carey wrote that Donne in this same letter is in effect "scrutinizing" his reader while the reader reads. This is,

> for Donne's period, a distinctly sophisticated account of the reading process. Instead of the reader reading the written page, the written page reads the reader, looking in through whatever 'doore' into his mind the reader chooses to open, and eliciting so much of his character as, in his interpretation of the written page, he reveals.[10]

The "me" delivered in these letters was projected both in relation to events that surrounded Donne (whether recounted, alluded to, or pointedly omitted from mention) and in consideration for his correspondent's concerns and expectations. These rhetorical points gave his letters their formal structure and their peculiar expression of his character, his "soul." In another letter, he wrote:

> I make account that this writing of letters, when it is with any seriousness, is a kind of extasie, and a departure and secession and suspension of the soul, which doth then communicate it self to two bodies: And as I would every day provide for my souls last convoy, though I know not when I shall die; so for these extasies in letters, I oftentimes deliver my self over in writing when I know not when those letters shall be sent to you, and many times they never are, for I have a little satisfaction in seeing a letter written to you upon my table, though I meet no opportunity of sending it.[11]

Carey remarked on this passage as "a key paragraph for understanding the kind of letter Donne writes," noting that, "If letters are ecstasies, then the absence of news and the exclusion of other kinds of

---

[9] Maurer, "Poetical Familiarity of Donne's Letters," 184.

[10] John Carey, "John Donne's Newsless Letters," *Essays and Studies* 34 (1981): 62; this essay contains important points about the letters that are ignored in Carey's *John Donne: Life, Mind and Art* (New York: Oxford Univ. Press, 1980).

[11] Donne to Goodyer, n.d.; *Letters to Severall Persons of Honour (1651)*, 11.

impersonal subject matter becomes no more than what is expected."[12] Donne's letters had substantial intention as expressions of his soul even before they were sent; and they did not need even to have been sent to fulfill this purpose. The soul thus projected was intended to be a communicable imprint of his person and situation, an intimate cross section of his presence that, if sent and if received, could at a distance mediate between, and be simultaneously experienced by, himself and someone else.

In this intention Donne was participating in a long tradition, from antiquity through the Renaissance, in which familiar letters were conceived as antidotes for absence, creating an illusion of the writer's presence as a vehicle for the union of friends' souls. Seminal in the tradition was St. Paul's comment in 1 Corinthians 5:3 that through a letter he could be "absent in body, but present in spirit."[13] Donne's craft of writing letters was a product of his having studied this tradition, on the assumption that "No other kinde of conveyance is better for knowledge, or love." He implied his conversance with epistolary literature in one letter that listed and characterized many different examples of published letters: the letters of the

---

[12] Carey, "Donne's Newsless Letters," 55.

[13] On the development of a theoretical tradition of epistolography, beginning with the first century Greek treatise *On Style*, influential in the Renaissance, see the edition and translation by R. V. Young and M. Thomas Hester of Justus Lipsius' *Principles of Letter-Writing: a Bilingual Text of* Justi Lipsi Epistolica Institutio (Carbondale and Edwardsville: Southern Illinois Univ. Press, 1996), xix-xxvi. Especially significant for the reading of Donne's letters is the definition of the letter by Lipsius (published in 1591): "a message of the mind written to someone who is absent or regarded as absent" (9). See also A. R. Littlewood, "An 'Ikon of the Soul': the Byzantine Letter," *Visible Language* 10 (1976): 216, quoting a letter from a tenth century monk, participating in the same tradition, in which letters are described as "comfort and consolation for friends who are separated, since they offer, when we read them, an illusion of the presence of what our mind desires. For this reason the man who called letters 'ikons of the absent' was perhaps right, since he who reads a letter sent by a friend has at the very moment of receiving and opening it filled his yearning soul with unsullied joy, because of the appearance that he is engaging in converse with his friend." Donne's studies in monastic writings of the tenth century and earlier are mentioned in two undated letters to Goodyer, *Letters to Severall Persons of Honour (1651)*, 33 and 48.

apostles; the letters of Brutus, Seneca, Pliny, and Cicero; the letters of Jesuit missionaries, from the east and from the west; and the abundant letters of Renaissance Italians, "which are most discursive, and think the world owes them all welcome."[14] However, one Italian letter writer in particular seems to have influenced Donne.

In 1537, Aretino became the first writer to publish an edition of his own letters in a vernacular language. Aretino's biographer and translator, Thomas C. Chubb, remarked that the six volumes of his letters constitute "approximately 4,000 pages of begging, fawning, and flattering, which are now, as befits the work of one who was intrinsically a journalist, just about as dead as last month's newspapers."[15] To Chubb's estimation of Aretino's dullness may be compared Carey's judgment of Donne's letters as "extremely dull—indeed, perversely and elaborately dull in a way which, we feel, the letters of a great poet have no right to be." Carey went on to argue

[14] Donne to Goodyer, n.d.; *Letters to Severall Persons of Honour (1651)*, 105-6. Concerning Italian letters, Donne here attributed to Montaigne a report of having seen four hundred volumes of them. What Montaigne actually said (in his essay "A Consideration upon Cicero") was: "The Italians are great Printers of Epistles, whereof I thinke I have a hundred severall Volumes"; *The Essayes of Michael Lord of Montaigne*, trans. John Florio, (London: J. M. Dent, 1928), 1: 268. On the abundance of Renaissance Italian letters, see Cecil H. Clough, "The Cult of Antiquity: Letters and Letter Collections," *Cultural Aspects of the Italian Renaissance: Essays in Honour of Paul Oskar Kristeller*, ed. C. H. Clough (Manchester: Manchester Univ. Press, 1976), 33-67.

Despite Donne's obvious awareness of the epistolary tradition, including such theoretical work as the *Opus de Conscribendis Epistolis* of Erasmus, Carey found that Donne's letter writing departed from both Cicero and Seneca, "the two chief models"; and from such letter-writing manuals as William Fulwood's *The Enemie of Idleness* (1568) and Angel Day's *The English Secretorie* (1586): "Whatever else we may think of Donne's letters, a comparison of them with the models his culture made available only reinforces our impression of his originality"; "Donne's Newsless Letters," 54.

[15] Chubb, *Aretino: Scourge of Princes* (New York: Reynal & Hitchcock, 1940), 356. Chubb's *Letters of Pietro Aretino* ([Hamden, Conn.:] Archon Books, 1967) presented his translations of a mere 261 Aretino letters. See also *Aretino: Selected Letters*, trans. George Bull (Harmondsworth: Penguin Books, 1976), translating 95 of the letters, some not included in Chubb's larger edition.

that the dullness of Donne's letters "was intended by Donne as a highly specialized and functional sort of dullness, based on imaginative theories which tie in closely with his poems."[16] Carey did not notice that these imaginative theories of Donne's are also in direct or obverse relation to certain theories set forth or embodied in the letters of Aretino. The volumes of Aretino's *Lettere* were in one sense a register of just the kinds of letters Donne told Goodyer he disdained or confessed his inability to compose. Aretino wrote habitually in tribute and in self-interest, in cheerful or grudging recompense; frank letters of commerce, testimonials of a kind of affection and provokers of it, justifying a habit and profession of writing and venting utterances of designed meditation by the eloquent son of a cobbler from Arezzo. Aretino's letters were emphatically neither above nor beneath such offices; yet Donne seems not only to have admired them but partly to have imitated them. These are letters of all kinds, "conveyances and deliverers" of Aretino to recipients who were targeted as friends, advisees, debtors, benefactors, or beadsmen. Aretino would open any door, it seems, and his letters would look in upon anyone.

Applied techniques for self-promotion, the *Lettere* were conceived as parts of a literary whole even prior to their publication as an epistolary. They were not an accrued record of incidents, nor were they published primarily as biographical documents. In book form they were grouped not chronologically but according to themes and for rhetorical effects. Donne evidently found Aretino's techniques of self-promotion through self-representation in the *Lettere* at once repugnant for their opportunism and fascinating for their brilliant rhetoric of occasion and audience, intensifying the presence of their absent author. In a related way, Donne's letters (as Carey observed) display an "almost pathological self-absorption," often dwelling with patient concentration on his own isolation, transmitting "the self-involved windings of his own consciousness."[17] Maurer commented that the self-possession and alienation often expressed in Donne's letters constitute

> what we can call his familiarity, what he himself often
> called his importunity—his ability to impress the image

---

[16] "Donne's Newsless Letters," 45.

[17] Ibid., 49, 65.

of himself as letter-writer on his reader. That sensibility
is the source of his power to dramatize and manipulate.[18]

Aretino had preceded Donne in these techniques.
Donne probably relished the many letters expressing Aretino's
original and seminal art criticism, especially concerning portraiture.
Donne's own penchant for commissioning portraits throughout his
life, like his collection of paintings and his particular interest in Titian, all seem related to his interest in Aretino. The *Lettere* present
their author as a set of assorted personae: "public and semi-private
masks," exchanged through shifts of scene or tone: "an articulate
diplomat and a bantering friend, a poor honest worker and a hope-
less spendthrift, a tender father and a formidable enemy." These
"paradoxical fragments" do not make up a whole person, but instead seem designed to be associated in clusters around the mottoes
that Aretino assigned to his medals, title-page designs, and portraits—painted by Titian and others—self-promoting phrases that
"lucidly convey the roles, or personae, which Aretino was eager to
assume." Through these mottoes, "Aretino affirmed the rhetorical
power of the portrait," and he treated each of his own portraits as
"an icon, which directly addresses, and even threatens the viewer."
Together with the letters, "the portraits and their accompanying
verse express Aretino's changing persona."[19]
    Raymond B. Waddington has discussed the achievement of
Aretino—not only through publication of his letters, but also
through commissioning these medals, title-page designs, and portraits adorned with mottoes—in creating the modern role of "the
author as personality or celebrity," someone "whose newest publication is read eagerly more because of who wrote it than what it is."[20]
The *Lettere* along with the portraits thus gave rise to Aretino's self-
trumpeted reputation as "*il flagello dei principi*" (the scourge of
princes); "*oracolo della verità*" (oracle of the truth); and "*segretario
del mondo*" (secretary of the world). Donne's portraits and mottoes,
in their profusion as well as in their designs as *imprese*, serve some

---

[18] "Donne's Familiar Letters," 199.
[19] Lora Ann Palladino, "Pietro Aretino: Orator and Art Theorist"
(Yale Univ. dissertation, 1981), ix, 19, and 170-1.
[20] "A Satirist's *Impresa*: The Medals of Pietro Aretino," *Renaissance
Quarterly* 42 (1989): 657.

parallel purposes. Prefaced to his *Metempsychosis* Donne set his picture, and it continued to preface many editions of his writings. As the sheer quantity and often the particular characteristics of manuscript versions of Donne's writings suggest, he was among the first examples of an English author whose work was celebrated as the product of a famous, even notorious personality. And although Donne seems never to have collected his own letters for publication, they do exhibit some of the qualities apparent in Aretino's.

Aretino's letters frequently mention his own art collection, including paintings by Titian, Tintoretto, Parmigianino, Vasari, and others, maintained in the manner of a modern art gallery, complete with receptions and promotions of new work by young artists.[21] After early education at an art school in Perugia, Aretino had been friendly at Rome in 1516 not only with Raphael but evidently also with the more standoffish Michelangelo.[22] When he came to live at Venice in 1527, Aretino immediately sought out Titian, for the purpose of having himself painted by the foremost portrait artist of the day (much as Donne would later commission Nicholas Hilliard and/or Isaac Oliver in England). Moreover, Aretino theorized a relation between literature and art in portraiture: "a symbiotic union of literature and likenesses." With the help of artist friends like Marcantonio Raimondi, Sebastiano del Piombo, and Titian, Aretino disseminated his own letters and portraits matched with mottoes and poems "to endow these faces with a voice— symbolically, the intellect and soul."[23]

In particular, through a kind of symbiosis in Aretino's promotion of Titian's portraiture over a period of years, in both letters and in sonnets written to be read while viewing the portraits, Aretino has been credited with introducing a new approach to the theory of portraiture, one that used ecphrastic methods formerly applied only

---

[21] Palladino, "Pietro Aretino: Orator and Art Theorist," 319ff.

[22] Aretino boasted in his letters that Raphael, before his early death in 1520, "used to consult him about his works before putting them on display"; Christopher Cairns, *Pietro Aretino and the Republic of Venice: Researches on Aretino and his Circle in Venice* (Florence: Leo S. Olschke Editore, 1985), 237-8. Despite his warm relations with many other great artists, Aretino was never able to obtain from Michelangelo any sample of his work.

[23] Palladino, "Pietro Aretino: Orator and Art Theorist," 319.

to "histories," paintings with narrative subjects. Aretino was the first art critic to draw attention to the identity of the portrait artist: "instead of just seeing a person portrayed, Aretino's readers began to think about how Titian represented this person."[24] Donne strikes a similar note in a letter to Christopher Brooke:

> a hand, or eye
> By *Hilliard* drawne, is worth an history
> By a worse painter made.[25]

Like Aretino, Donne not only commissioned portraits by the foremost artists in the genre; at his death, he owned a collection of more than twenty sixteenth- and seventeenth-century pictures, mainly portraits and sacred art, including several paintings or copies of paintings by European masters. Among these perhaps the most impressive was a big one of three life-sized figures by Titian, described in Donne's will as "the picture of the Blessed Virgin Mary which hangs in the little dining-chamber." This picture he bequeathed to his friend James Hay, Earl of Carlisle, who later gave it to King Charles I. Already in Donne's younger years, to acquire a Titian was to spend a small fortune; such costs grew even higher toward the end of his life. Very few people in England owned a Titian. Donne's quasi-royal bounty in dealings over this picture (and others) should be seen as one largely disregarded element in what became known as his "universall Monarchy of wit."[26]

---

[24] Luba Freedman, *Titian's Portraits Through Aretino's Lens* (Univ. Park: Univ. of Pennsylvania Press, 1995), ix and 15.

[25] Shawcross, *Complete Poetry of Donne*, 189. Donne's "Satyre IV," written at about the same time, made reference to Albrecht Dürer's "rules" for proportionate drawings of human bodies; ibid., 33. Donne was "the first English poet to show awareness of the work of Hilliard and Dürer"; W. Milgate, "Dr. Donne's Art Gallery," *Notes and Queries* 194 (1949): 319.

[26] When and where Donne acquired his Titian we do not know, although some evidence would suggest as most likely the period Donne spent in Venice in late 1605 and early 1606, unless (as seems quite possible) he had also made an earlier visit to Venice. In any case, the painting does not appear to have survived among extant works of Titian. It was last described in a 1639 catalog of the King's artwork as "done by Titian; being our Lady, and Christ, and St. John, half figures, as big as the life . . . being

Given the rigid protocols for patronage all the Courts of Europe observed, only in Venice could Aretino and Titian have carried out their mutually self-promoting enterprise in literature and art; and their presence in the Republic of Venice itself focuses attention on several further key elements in their attraction for Donne. In fact, the feature of Aretino's *Lettere* that may most have appealed to Donne is their rather tartly Venetian attitude toward Courts and courtiers. Aretino's experience of courtiers began with the papal Court of Leo X, where he was a younger contemporary of Baldassare Castiglione, then serving as ambassador for the Duke of Urbino. At the time, Aretino was considerably beneath Castiglione in status, serving as an assistant to the Roman banker Agostino Chigi. Nevertheless, he may well then or soon after have seen a manuscript copy of Castiglione's nostalgic masterpiece, *Il Libro del Cortegiano*, which idealized turn-of-the-century Urbino and was circulating at the papal Court as early as 1516 (though it was not published until twelve years later). Aretino subsequently established himself as a satirist in Rome through his iconoclastic *pasquinate* and sonnets ridiculing the Roman Court, especially the College of Cardinals and their choice of a new pope at the consistory in 1522.

Aretino's experiences under Popes Leo X and his successor Adrian VI were quite a contrast from Castiglione's at Urbino. The sophisticated Medici pope could tolerate Aretino's satire, issued in soothsaying pamphlets and macaronic poems. But with the advent of the dour Adrian, Aretino began an enforced exile from the papal Court. In 1525, during an uneasy sojourn at the Court of the Duke of Mantua, Aretino took aim at Castiglione's "perfect courtier" in his earliest comedy, *La Cortigiana*. This play, in part a satirical response to Castiglione's similarly titled dialogue, took a less idealistic view of courtiers, even before it was revised when, in 1527, Aretino finally settled in republican Venice, given sanctuary by the Senate

---

in a carved gilded frame, and was given heretofore to his Majesty by my Lord of Carlisle, who had it of Dr Donn"; Milgate, "Dr. Donne's Art Gallery," 318. Donne's will, largely devoted to the bequeathal of his pictures, and making mention of over twenty specific works as well as unspecified others, is in Bald, *John Donne: a Life*, 563-7. On Donne's "Monarchy of wit" see Carew's funeral poem, "An Elegie upon the death of the Deane of Pauls, Dr. Iohn Donne," in Shawcross, *Complete Poetry of Donne*, 3-5.

and liberated from all the Courts of princes. Aretino's 1538 dialogue, *Ragionamento delle Corti*, was an open attack on all Courts, in which the traits attributed to courtiers were made with mockery deliberately to "echo the traits of Castiglione's courtier."[27]

By this time his letter-writing had long since been a stream of anti-Court sentiment that continued for the rest of his life, along with his other writings from Venice building a public relations monument that made him a legend in his own time.[28] When Aretino revised his play *La Cortigiana* for re-publication at Venice in 1534, he inserted material seemingly alluding to his own fortunate decision to come to Venice from Mantua. In the revised play a courtier named Flaminio, faced with the same decision, denounces the viciousness of the Roman Court and extols Venice as the European home of justice, the one true "Holy City."[29] Aretino's letter to the Doge of Venice, Andrea Gritti, spoke in similar terms, as always promoting Aretino's own image.[30]

In the 1590s Donne certainly had reason to share the bad opinion of Courts he found in Aretino's *Lettere*, although the injustice most keenly felt by Donne and his family had not been dealt by the courtiers, priests, or Pope of Rome. Instead it was the Court of Elizabeth that bore the brunt of Donne's censure, beginning in his

---

[27] Cairns, *Pietro Aretino and the Republic of Venice*, 47.

[28] Ibid., 33-4.

[29] Quoted in Chubb, *Aretino: Scourge of Princes*, 167: "Only in Venice does justice hold the scales with an even balance. There only, fear of disgrace does not force you to adore someone who was in the gutter only yesterday. Surely she is a Holy City and the Earthly Paradise." Cf. Cairns, *Pietro Aretino and the Republic of Venice*, 74.

[30] "I, who in the freedom of this State have succeeded in learning to be free, renounce the Court for ever and ever, and I build here an everlasting tabernacle for the years that are left me. For here treachery has no place, here reigns neither the cruelty of harlots nor the insolence of the effeminate, here there is no theft, or violence, or murder . . . . Venice embraces Italy when others shun her, and upholds her when others abase her; she feeds her when others starve her; she shelters her when others hunt her down, and, comforting her in her tribulations, sustains her with charity and love . . . . She is a reproach to Rome; for here, no one can tyrannize over others or seeks to do so, while there, freedom has been enslaved by the priests"; Aretino to Andrea Gritti, Doge of Venice, 1530; Bull, *Aretino: Selected Letters*, 65-6.

Satyres, verse letters, and letters in prose, continuing in the *Metempsychosis* (written near the end of Elizabeth's reign) and (during in the earlier reign of King James) in *The Courtier's Library* and *Ignatius His Conclave*. The last of these, of course, includes Aretino explicitly in the satire, as does "Satyre IV." In both cases he appears in his best-known role as pornographer, but in both cases he also participates in Donne's subversive treatment of the Court and courtiers. A general and consistent scorn characterizes every single reference to the Court not only in Donne's poems but in his other writings up to 1612. Donne's general attitude toward the Court in this period is perhaps best summed up in his comment about Castiglione in "Satyre V": "hee being understood May make good Courtiers, but who Courtiers good?" What the satirist clearly implies is that neither Castiglione nor anyone else can make them good; in other words, generally speaking, courtiers are not good. The unremitting severity in Donne's moral judgment of courtiers is much in the same vein as Aretino's.

Moreover, like Aretino, Donne in this connection seems to have held the Republic of Venice in special regard. His trip to Venice in 1605-1606 was, as I have suggested, likely not his first visit there. The 1605 trip may well have been a return at least partly motivated by a wish to explore, perhaps at the invitation of Henry Wotton, whether he might relocate. While Donne was at Wotton's house the long-simmering conflict between Venice and the papal Court broke out with climactic ferocity, the Pope excommunicating all the members of the Senate and forbidding the Venetian clergy to administer the sacraments within Venetian territory—the infamous and ill-advised "papal interdict."

Back in England by the spring of 1606, Donne's keen interest in the republican independence of Venice led to his careful study of the complete propaganda war then ongoing between Rome's Jesuit controversialists and the Republic's chief counselor Paolo Sarpi. In *Pseudo-Martyr* Donne demonstrated his mastery of this literature and his complete satisfaction both with the arguments of Sarpi and with their victory in the conflict. Thereafter, to his dying day, Donne honored Sarpi's portrait prominently in his home, displaying it in his parlor. According to Walton, he had met Sarpi on one of his trips to Venice. Certainly in relation to the papal Court,

Sarpi may be said to have inherited Aretino's title as "*il flagello dei principi.*"

One further element in Donne's attraction to Aretino's letters was their Erasmian flavor, a way of thinking more endemic to Venice than to any other Italian city. At Venice had grown a virtual cult of patrician Erasmian enthusiasts, the core consituency supporting publication of the Aldine editions of Erasmus's writings. In a letter of 1538, Aretino mentioned Erasmus as one who

> has enlarged the confines of the human mind and who with no model other than himself is for all mankind the only exemplar of himself. There is no one to compare him with, for he was a strong fountain of speech, a broad river of intellect, and an immense sea of literature; therefore his stature is such as to defy description.[31]

The roots of this enthusiasm were entwined with the early roots of Catholic reform in Italy, especially through the work of the Venetian noble ecclesiastic Gasparo Contarini, who led the movement during the 1530s.

Aretino has been called an "unlikely bedfellow" in relation to Erasmus, but in fact during the 1530s he did align himself with members of Contarini's group, publishing eight books of devotional prose by 1542.[32] It was during this period that St. Ignatius Loyola, himself still sympathetic to Erasmus, sojourned in Venice, administered the spiritual exercises to Contarini, and was in 1537 joined, for several months of charitable service to the dying in the hospitals of Venice, by the men who would later become the nine original Jesuits. Although Aretino's associations cannot be traced directly to the good works of the Jesuits, he did have contacts with several of the Venetian nobility close to Loyola. These activities evidence his awareness of the spiritual tension prevailing in Italy just prior to the advent of the Council of Trent and suggest his inclination to the course proposed by the Erasmians among the reformers. In his de-

---

[31] Aretino to Giambattista Salis Grisone, 6 June 1538; ibid., 175.

[32] *La Passione di Giesù* (1534), *I Quattro Libri de la Humanita di Cristo* (1535), *Gli Sette Salmi di Penitenza* (1536), *Il Genesi, con la Visione di Noè, ne la Quale Vede I Misteri del Testamento Vecchio e del Nuovo* (1538), *Vita di Maria Vergine* (1539), *Vita di Caterina Vergine e Martire* (1540), and *Vita di san Tomaso, Signor d'Aquino* (1543).

votional books Aretino expressed a confessional point of view akin to that of Erasmus. He was quite Catholic but torn, along with many members of his generation, forced by events to choose between Lutheran notions of "individual conscience" and "the harsh rigour of the militant Counter-reformation." Aretino's devotional writings attempt to hold on to what he presents as "the calm and qualified good sense of a moderate and Erasmian middle way."[33]

To conclude, Donne's early interest in Aretino's letters probably focused on their style of artful self-presentation, including their interest in portraiture; on their satirical attitude toward Courts and courtiers; on their presentation of the art and culture of Venice, in particular of the portraits and other paintings of Titian; and on their generally Erasmian tone, especially in religious matters. These are all areas in which Donne showed particular interest throughout his life, interest that to some extent may well have been shaped by his early reading of Aretino.

Bentley College

---

[33] Cairns, *Pietro Aretino and the Republic of Venice*, 8. The phrase "unlikely bedfellows" is also in Cairns (ibid., 10).

The Ovidian Underworld in *Othello* 3.3

PAMELA ROYSTON MACFIE

"Methought the billows spoke, and told me of it"
— *The Tempest*, 3.3.96

A T the center of *Othello*, as the Moor conveys his unbending determination to pursue vengeance, Shakespeare employs an extended simile that is haunted by several prior voices. The moment advanced by the simile is crucial. It prefaces Othello's pledge, sworn upon an aloof and impenetrable "marble heaven" (3.3.460),[1] that he will do the bidding of murder rather than love; simultaneously, the simile defines Othello's surrender to the fatal imprecations of Iago. With the simile, then, Shakespeare marks that moment in which the play turns fully to tragedy. But he also does something more. Informed not merely by phrases from Pliny's *Natural History*, but also by images from Ovid's *Tristia* and Marlowe's *Hero and Leander*, Othello's extended simile evokes the pathos of the underworld as well as the absolutism of his vengeance.

Othello's recourse to similetic comparison is prompted by Iago's counsel for "patience" (an ironic counsel for suffering as well as for resignation and forbearance)[2] and by Iago's intimation that Othello's "mind perhaps may change" (3.3.452). Othello has just urged Iago to note: "All my fond love thus do I blow to heaven" (3.3.445). In the succeeding line, which is significantly abrupted, Othello comments merely and succinctly upon his love: "'Tis gone"

---

[1] All quotations from Shakespeare's works are from the second edition of *The Riverside Shakespeare*, ed. G. Blakemore Evans et al. (Boston: Houghton Mifflin Company, 1997).

[2] The derivation of the English word patience from the Latin *patiens*, from the present participle of *pati*, to suffer, suggests the double meaning (*OED*).

(3.3.446). In spite of the monosyllabic certainty of this dismissal and the ritual force of Othello's subsequent invocation of Ate, the dark spirit of vengeance whom Othello summons from a Stygian cave (3.3.447), Iago still tests Othello's resolve. "Never, Iago," begins Othello's response to Iago's proposal that his mind may change. Following the absolute negative, which opens Othello's line with an emphatic trochee, the extended simile appears:

> Never, Iago. Like to the Pontic Sea,
> Whose icy current and compulsive course
> Nev'r [feels] retiring ebb, but keeps due on
> To the Propontic and the Hellespont,
> Even so my bloody thoughts, with violent pace,
> Shall nev'r look back, nev'r ebb to humble love,
> Till that a capable and wide revenge
> Swallow them up. Now by yond marble heaven,
> In the due reverence of a sacred vow
> I here engage my words. (3.3.453-62)[3]

On the most immediate level, Othello's comparison of his "bloody thoughts" to the "icy current and compulsive course" of the Pontic Sea conveys the relentless energy that characterizes his turn to vengeance. Othello cites the characteristics for which the Pontic Sea was infamous, its preternatural cold and swift, treacherous cur-

---

[3] Occupying lines 453-60, the simile prefacing Othello's reference to "yond marble heaven" does not appear in the first Quarto. Assessments of the appropriateness of the lines have varied greatly. Pope contended that the simile was omitted in the first Quarto because it could only stand "as an unnatural excursion in this place." Swinburne, quite differently, described the simile as "one of the most precious jewels that ever the prodigal afterthought of a great poet bestowed upon the rapture of his readers." For Swinburne, Othello's elaboration of the simile seemed fully in place and character: "In other lips, indeed, than Othello's, at the crowning minute of culminant agony, the rush of imaginative reminiscence which brings back upon his eyes and ears the lightning foam and tideless thunder of the Pontic sea might seem a thing less natural than sublime. But Othello has the passion of a poet closed in, as it were, and shut up behind the passion of a hero." These comments are cited from the notes to lines 460-7 in the 1974 reprint of M. R. Ridley's 1958 Arden edition of *Othello* (London: Methuen, 1974), 121. Ridley provides further discussion of the possible status of these lines as a later addition in "Appendix A," 200.

rents, as markers of his murderous determination. In enjambed lines that reach a breathless close in the ominous place-name of the "Hellespont," Othello's words, like his thoughts, mimic the ceaseless flow of the Black Sea; the trajectory of this flow, and of Othello's thoughts, is of course the trajectory of death.

Numerous commentators have noted that Othello's words closely follow Pliny's *Historia Naturalis* 2.100.219: "Et Pontus semper extra meat in Propontidem, introrsus in Pontum numquam refluo mari."[4] It is doubtful, though, that Shakespeare turns to Pliny's Latin here. Philemon Holland's English translation of this passage in his *Natural History*, "And the sea Pontus evermore floweth and runneth out into Propontis, but the sea never retireth back againe within Pontus,"[5] closely anticipates several phrases within Othello's rhetorical display. Like Holland, Shakespeare incorporates some form of the word "retire" within his description of the sea-currents; like Holland, he prefaces "retiring" (in Holland, "retireth") with "never"; like Holland, he pursues the Pontic Sea's current all the way to the Propontic Sea of Marmora, located between the Black Sea and the Aegean. In 4.13.93 of the *Historia*, Pliny reconsiders the energy and force of these currents, noting (as Holland translates): "Out of Pontus the sea always floweth, and never ebbeth again." From the larger context of Holland's translation of Pliny 4.13.93-5, as Sanders points out (132), Shakespeare would seem to echo not only the word "ebb," but also the words "icy," "wide," and the phrase "compulsive course."

In spite of these instances of verbal and figurative resonance, several critics, including Charles and Michelle Martindale, assert that Shakespeare "is not evoking Pliny but high classical epic and

---

[4] This citation from Pliny is to the Loeb Library edition of H. Rackham, *Natural History* (Cambridge, MA: Harvard Univ. Press, 1949), volume 1, 348. References to Shakespeare's apparent indebtedness here to Pliny may be found in J. A. K. Thomson, *Shakespeare and the Classics* (Bristol: J. W. Arrowsmith, Ltd., 1952), 127; Norman Sanders's New Cambridge Shakespeare edition of *Othello* (Cambridge: Cambridge Univ. Press, 1984), 132; and Charles and Michelle Martindale, *Shakespeare and the Uses of Antiquity: An Introductory Essay* (London: Routledge, 1990), 36.

[5] Cited from Thomson (127), who provides a compelling argument that Shakespeare would not have consulted Pliny's Latin text.

tragedy" (36). Gordon Braden argues that Shakespeare recalls
Pliny's description in Othello's speech because of a specific precedent in Seneca's *Medea*; Shakespeare was clearly familiar with the
Senecan passage in question, for he closely echoes its words and
ideas in *King John* 2.1.451-5.[6] In the passage, Medea, anticipating
Othello, aligns herself with nature's most expansive and destructive
forces in order to embrace what Braden calls "an ideal of murderous
constancy" (176):

> While the pole turns the dry arctic bears and the rivers
> fall into the Pontus, never will my furor cease in its pun-
> ishing, but will always increase. What savagery of beasts,
> what Scylla, what Charybdis swallowing the Ausonian
> and Sicilian sea, or what Etna crushing the breathing
> Titan will burn with such threats? Not the swift river,
> nor the stormy sea or Pontus raging from the northwest
> wind or the power of fires fanned by the tempest can
> hold back my force and anger: I will destroy and over-
> turn everything. (*Medea* 404-14)[7]

For Braden, the affective dynamics of the Senecan passage, which
incidentally recalls Pliny's geography, inform not merely Othello's
speech in 3.3, but, finally, Shakespeare's play at large (176-7).

---

[6] Gordon Braden, *Renaissance Tragedy and the Senecan Tradition:
Anger's Privilege* (New Haven: Yale Univ. Press, 1985), 176.
[7] This passage from Seneca's *Medea* (404-14) is cited from Braden,
176 and, in the body of this essay, from Braden's translation. Braden uses
the edition of the *Medea* found in *L. Annaei Senecae Tragoediae*, ed.
Giancarlo Giardina (Bologna, 1966):

> dum siccas polus
> uersabit Arctos, flumina in Pontum cadent,
> numquam meus cessabit in poenas furor
> crescetque semper--quae ferarum immanitas,
> quae Scylla, quae Charybdis ausonium mare
> siculumque sorbens quaeue anhelantem premens
> Titana tantis Aetna feruebit minis?
> non rapidus amnis, non procellosum mare
> Pontusue coro saeuus aut uis ignium
> adiuta flatu possit inhibere impetum
> irasque nostras: sternam et euertam omnia.

Charles and Michelle Martindale similarly find that the significance of Shakespeare's echo of Pliny inheres in that echo's creation of certain rhetorical and heroic effects. The Martindales note Shakespeare's unusual repetition of highly similar words within the formally constructed simile and propose that Othello endeavors in elevated, architectonic speech to carry himself beyond any vicissitude—of feeling *or* language—that might threaten or qualify his resolve. Emphasizing the determinedly constructed absolutism of Othello's words, the Martindales finally conclude not merely that Othello's speech is Senecan in style and feeling; they conclude also that "the speech is too weighty for Ovid" (36).

Yet Ovid meditates in the *Tristia* on the very characteristics of the Pontic sea that initiate Othello's speech. And though there is no coincidence of style between Ovid's geographical descriptions and Othello's, there is, I contend, a portentous coincidence of atmosphere. Throughout the poems in the *Tristia*, Ovid depicts the Pontic region as if it were an alternative underworld[8] (as he does in *Epistulae ex Pontus* 1.8.27 and 4.9.74, though scholars have discovered no evidence that Shakespeare knew this work). This association of the Pontic sea with the region of the dead may well subtend Othello's evocation of Ate's infernal cell in one breath (3.3.447) and the Pontic sea's "icy current" (3.3.454) in the next.

In *Tristia* 5.9.19-20, remembering how his exile began with his shipwreck in the Pontic sea, Ovid recalls that, as he "swam in [those] savage seas," a nameless friend "alone didst recall [him] half lifeless from the Stygian waters" ("nec dederit nanti per freta saeva manum, / seminecem Stygia revocasti solus ab unda").[9] At the opening of *Tristia* 5.10.1-2, characterizing the evils of Tomis, the exiled poet notes that he has witnessed on three different occasions the frigid waters by the Pontus's shore turn to ice: "Ut sumus in Ponto, ter frigore constitit Hister, / facta esta Euxini dura ter unda maris." In this detail, Ovid follows several ancient precedents, including that of Pliny (*Historia Naturalis* 4.12.87), which also de-

---

[8] For a discussion of this topos across several Ovidian texts, see Gareth D. Williams, *Banished Voices: Readings in Ovid's Exile Poetry* (Cambridge: Cambridge Univ. Press, 1994), 12-22.

[9] Citations of Ovid's *Tristia* are to the Loeb Library edition of Arthur Leslie Wheeler (Cambridge, MA: Harvard Univ. Press, 1939); translations of the *Tristia* are also from Wheeler.

scribe the streams in the Pontic region, and even the Pontic sea itself, as so cold that they freeze over completely.[10] As Gareth Williams notes (10), such reports inspired skepticism among such writers as Gellius, but the image of the freezing sea nonetheless became a paradigmatic feature of the Pontic region in Latin poetry (cf. Virgil, *Georgics* 3.360-2).

In no less than six passages in the *Tristia*, Ovid offers variations upon this motif: in 2.187-96, 3.10.25-50, 4.4.55-8, 5.2.64, 5.10.1-2, and 5.13.21. Cumulatively, Ovid's descriptions of the cold shores and sea of Pontus define a place of climatic and geographic extremity alike: an otherworldly void unvisited by any movement except that of the storm-tossed water. Ovid laments in *Tristia* 4.4.55-8:

> frigida me cohibent Euxini litora Ponti:
> dictus ab antiquis Axenus ille fuit.
> nam neque iactantur moderatis aequora ventis,
> nec placidos portus hospita navis adit.

> (The cold shores of the Pontus Euxinus keep me; by men of old it was called Axenus. For its waters are tossed by no moderate winds and there are no quiet harbors visited by foreign ships.)

For Ovid, the experience of exile is the experience of living death. Ovid's early association of the underworld with unbearable and unrelenting cold in *Metamorphoses* 4.436 ("pallor hiemsque tenent late loca senta"[11]) anticipates and finally reinforces his association in the *Tristia* of the cold waters of the Pontic sea with the realm and the torments of the dead.

Ovid muses somewhat differently on the image of the Pontus sealed in ice in *Tristia* 3.10.41-4. There, he briefly invokes Leander: "If thou, Leander, hadst once had such a sea, thy death would not have been a charge against the narrow waters" ("si tibi tale fretum quondam, Leandre, fuisset, / non foret angustae mors tua crimen aquae"). A witty irony, typical of Ovid, inheres in this address. Viewed from one perspective, the frozen expanse of the Pontus

---

[10] Williams (10) also cites the precedents of Herodotus (4.28) and Strabo (7.3.18) for accounts of the frozen Pontic sea.

[11] This citation of Ovid's *Metamorphoses* is to the Loeb Library edition of Frank Justus Miller (Cambridge, MA: Harvard Univ. Press, 1977).

conjures associations of the unnatural cold of the underworld; viewed from another, the same expanse appears to offer an antidote to the watery surge that drowned Leander. Ovid of course plays with impossibility here. Leander is invoked from the grave. The association of the waters of the Pontus and the Hellespont with Leander's cold death cannot be exorcised. The Hellespont, as any reader of Ovid or Musaeus knows, is the fatal medium of the lovers' separation.

If Shakespeare, as he composed Othello's speech, reread or re-membered Ovid's several meditations on the Pontus's cold waters in the *Tristia*, Ovid's reference to Leander therein may subtly have motivated him to include the Hellespont as the third and final term within Othello's tracking of the Pontus's irresistible flow. Othello's geographical citations of the Pontic Sea and the Propontic rebound to Pliny (and/or Holland's translation of Pliny), but his reference to the Hellespont finds no precedent in such a source. Completing a series of riddling repetitions (all of which effect variations on the Latin word, Pontus, naming the Black Sea), the reference to the Hellespont is the most darkly suggestive reference in the series. Different from the first references, the Hellespont evokes not merely a place of marine danger and cold; it also evokes a place haunted by particular kinds of loss. As Othello's triple naming of place tracks the expanding course of the cold sea-current, his words carry his thoughts to a realm that is mythic and poetic, rather than merely geographic. Literally, the naming of Hellespont brings into view those dangerous straits that join the Propontic and Aegean Seas. Allusively, the Hellespont recalls the love-tragedy relayed by Ovid in *Heroides* 18 and 19 and, in due time, as Shakespeare knew well, by Christopher Marlowe.

Marlowe's *Hero and Leander*, which Shakespeare echoes in sev-eral works,[12] pursues the story of Ovid's and Musaeus's doomed

---

[12] Shakespeare most persistently references Marlowe's *Hero and Lean-der* in *As You Like It*, where, interestingly enough, in the midst of Touchstone's meditations on Arden, we encounter a reference in one breath to "honest Ovid [penning his *Tristia*] among the Goths" (3.3.8-9) and, in the next, to Marlowe's sudden death: that "great reckoning in a little room" (3.3.15). In *As You Like It*, Shakespeare refers explicitly to Marlowe's *Hero and Leander* when Rosalind ironically echoes Marlowe's identification of Hero as a "nun" (4.1.101) and when the love-lorn Phoebe

lovers from their overwhelming experience of "[love] . . . at first sight" (I.176),[13] through their awkward, sometimes comical courtship, to their love's violent consummation. Whether by artistic purpose or by the unexpected tragedy of the poet's death, Marlowe's *Hero and Leander* does not reach the narrative conclusion appointed by ancient literary tradition: Leander's death by drowning and Hero's subsequent suicide. Nonetheless, the poem is enfolded by death. Opening with a reference to the "Hellespont, guilty of true love's blood" (I.1), the poem closes with a reference to the underworld as ugly Night hurls "down to hell her loathsome carriage" (II.334). Arguably, Marlowe's opening line, "On Hellespont, guilty of true love's blood," stands as the most memorable naming of the Hellespont in early modern literature. Marlowe's description of the Hellespont as a place "guilty of true love's blood" lacks precedent in both his primary source, the late Alexandrian epyllion by Musaeus, and also his second source, Ovid's *Heroides* 18 and 19.

The lovers' Ovidian letters do, however, include several suggestive references to the storm-swollen body of water that bars their reunion. In *Heroides* 18.7-8, Leander characterizes the familiar waters as turbid and troubled with winds ("freta ventis turbida"[14]) even as the heavens grow black as pitch above them ("caelum pice nigrius"). Seventy lines later, Leander recalls in plaintive contrast how the same waters were calm, "the wave . . . radiant with the image of the reflected moon" ("unda repercussae radiabat imagine lunae," 77), during that night when he first swam to Hero. Finally, near the close of his letter, Leander pronounces the strait's associa-

---

formally invokes Marlowe immediately before she cites one of his poem's most famous lines: "Dead shepherd, now I find thy saw of might, / 'Who ever lov'd that lov'd not at first sight'" (3.5.81-2). Regarding Phoebe's citation, Charles Nicholl contends that it "is the only occasion in all Shakespeare's plays when he quotes and acknowledges—rather than just quietly borrowing—a line by a contemporary author"; see *The Reckoning: The Murder of Christopher Marlowe* (New York: Harcourt Brace and Company, 1992), 73.

[13] All quotations of Marlowe's *Hero and Leander* are from the Revels edition of Millar Maclure (London: Methuen and Co., Ltd., 1968).

[14] Citations of Ovid's *Heroides* are to the Loeb Library's second edition of G. P. Goold (Cambridge, MA: Harvard Univ. Press, 1977); translations are from Grant Showerman, also from this Loeb edition.

tion with death, tracing the etymology of its name and infamy back to the drowned maid, Helle, who fell into the sea from the back of a winged ram that she had mounted in an attempt to flee her murderous stepmother:

> fluctibus inmodicis Athamantidos aequora canent,
> vixque manet portu tuta carina suo;
> hoc mare, cum primum de virgine nomina mersa,
> quae tenet, est nanctum, tale fuisse puto.
> est satis amissa locus hic infamis ab Helle,
> utque mihi parcat, nomine crimen habet. (137-42)

In *Heroides* 19, Hero similarly muses upon the wind-stirred waves ("aut mare prospiciens odioso concita vento," 21). Like Leander, she also remembers how the strait came to possess its name. Hero considers that the storm's ceaseless surge of wave, wind, and rain derives either from the sorrow of Helle's mother, Nephele, or, quite differently, from the vengeance of her stepmother, Ino:

> forsitan ad pontum mater pia venerit Helles,
> mersaque roratis nata fleatur aquis—
> an mare ab inviso privignae nomine dictum
> vexat in aequoream versa noverca deam?
> non favet, ut nunc est, teneris locus iste puellis;
> hac Helle periit, hac ego laedor aqua. (123-8)

> (It may be the loving mother of Helle has come to the sea, and is lamenting in downpouring tears the drowning of her child—or is the step-dame, turned to a goddess of the waters, vexing the sea that is called by her step-child's hated name? This place, such as 'tis now, is aught but friendly to tender maids; by these waters Helle perished, by them my own affliction comes.)

According to Hero's troubled words in *Heroides* 19.123-8, the storm-tossed Hellespont is ambiguously and simultaneously inscribed by loss *and* vengeance, lamentation *and* curse, love *and* hatred.

A similar confluence of opposed meanings haunts Othello's declaration of murderous constancy. Invoking the Hellespont, Othello also summons (albeit unconsciously) poignant associations of love's loss as well as darker associations of jealous vengeance. A certain pathos clings to the word Hellespont, in Shakespeare as well as in Ovid. Though Othello's pronunciation of "the Hellespont" may extend a series of repetitions that endeavor to signify the utter lack of variance within his murderous thoughts, the word also unsettles the pattern he has insistently established. Naming the Hellespont, Othello names a place of love. The Hellespont, as several erotic remembrances in *Heroides* 18 make clear, is the medium of Leander's ecstatic passage to Hero as well as the site of his death.[15] For a fleeting moment, Othello's assertion of vengeance opens to evocations of longing and suffering, as well as to the possibility that love is remembered even in the pronouncement of its cancellation.

There are, then, several potentially Ovidian associations in *Othello* 3.3.453-62. Nonetheless, for Shakespeare, the crucial characterization of the Hellespont would finally seem to be that of Marlowe. Strategically situated and constructed, Marlowe's memorable opening line, unlike the more scattered and tangential musings of Ovid's Hero and Leander, offers an uncanny gloss upon the complexity of Othello's words. "On Hellespont, guilty of true love's blood" evinces what Patrick Cheney has identified as Marlowe's crucial definition of love: "true love originates in blood."[16] Marlowe presents to his readers (including Shakespeare) not merely that the Hellespont is "guilty of true love's blood" because, according to lit-

---

[15] One of the most elaborate of Leander's erotic reminiscences in *Heroides* 18 describes the preternatural calm of that moonlit night when he first swam to Hero (75-82). As the letter advances, Leander recalls the energy with which he stroked the tranquil deep and reimagines the intensity with which he might again ply the waters and come to rest in Hero (207-8). In lines 107-8, Leander endeavors to express the infinitude of ecstasy that he shared with Hero by musing upon the innumerable weeds of the Hellespontic sea. At the close of his letter, he dreams that he might be embraced alike by the sea and Hero's tender arms (217-8).

[16] See *Marlowe's Counterfeit Profession: Ovid, Spenser, Counternationhood* (Toronto: Univ. of Toronto Press, 1997), 242. Elaborating this point, Cheney writes further: "Hero and Leander are doomed from the start, and not simply by geography, but by nature—the nature of things, identified as the red stream of life flowing within the human frame. The oxymoronic pairing of *truth* with *guilt* is a Marlovian miniature at its most refined. What is true is what ruins; what we are born with annihilates us. Love destroys; blood kills" (242).

erary tradition, it has gathered Leander within its cold embrace and, as a consequence, inspired his beloved's suicide. Marlowe also presents the idea that "true love" is conceived and completed in "blood." In Marlowe's hands, who will present Hero and Leander's erotic consummation in terms of cruelty and violence (II.287-91), love and blood are coincident with one another.

It is precisely this dark association that Othello realizes in turning his thrice-repeated curse upon love, "blood, blood, blood" (3.3.451), into his triple-naming of those waters whose movement from "the Pontic sea . . . to the Propontic and the Hellespont" (3.3.453-6) signals death. Blood undergoes several transformations in Othello's words. The first transformation empties the word of its positive associations with life and passion and reduces it to an impious curse. The second turns the image of blood, by line 457 an image of murderous energy rather than passionate life, deadly cold.

Even as Othello's simile permits him to embrace an ideal of murderous necessity, it glances ahead to the consequences of such necessity's realization. When, too late, Othello discovers Desdemona's innocence and his own guilt, he returns to marine images of otherworldly cold and extremity. Describing the weapon that he will turn against himself, Othello notes that its strength derives from its immersion, just as its hot metal had been forged, in ice-cold water: "It was a sword of Spain, the ice-brook's temper" (5.2.253). Several lines later, employing the universal metaphor of life as a sea-journey, Othello conveys to Gratiano his fated terminus. Permitting his words and deeds, one last time, to follow the course of the sea, Othello identifies his "journey's end": "here is my butt / And very sea-mark of my utmost sail" (5.2.267-8). Othello's language here aspires to a beacon or similar landmark set upon the shore of death. The fatal implications of the Hellespont and its shore, which Ovid associates in *Heroides* 18 and 19 with the almost supernatural agency of Hero's lamp-lit tower, are literalized in Othello's preparation for suicide.[17]

Sea imagery, of course, appears throughout *Othello* as part of the symbolic backdrop to the problematic love of Desdemona and the Moor. A "desperate tempest" (2.1.21) off the coast of Cyprus

---

[17] Ovid variously presents Hero's lamp (and, by association, in certain instances, her tower) as a beacon that summons Leander to love and to death; see *Heroides* 18.85-92 and 105-6 and *Heroides* 19.33-6 and 151-2.

does not merely disable the Turkish fleet at the opening of Act 2; it also delays the arrival of Othello and, in this, thwarts his reunion with his bride. Several detailed descriptions of this "high-wrought flood" (2.1.2) dominate 2.1. In lines 12 through 17, the second gentleman describes how

> The chidden billow seems to pelt the clouds,
> The wind-shak'd surge, with high and monstrous mane,
> Seems to cast water on the burning Bear,
> And quench the guards of th' ever-fixed Pole;
> I never did like molestation view
> On the enchafed flood. (2.1.12-7)

This description presents a picture of the world turned upside-down, a world in which the very distinction between heaven and earth seems subject to dissolution. Some one hundred and seventy lines later, Othello, celebrating his reunion with Desdemona, offers his own version of this topos. Again, a tempest-tossed sea returns the world to primal chaos:

> If after every tempest come such calms,
> May the winds blow till they have waken'd death!
> And let the laboring bark climb hills of seas
> Olympus-high, and duck again as low
> As hell's from heaven! (2.1.185-9)

In each of these passages, Shakespeare, as several commentators have noted,[18] turns to Ovid, whose *Metamorphoses* provides a similarly rich description of the world turned upside-down. Golding's translation of the relevant passage in *Metamorphoses* 11 reads:

> One whyle as from a mountaynes toppe it seemed downe too
>   looke,
> Too vallyes and the depth of hell. Another whyle beset
> With swelling surges round about which neere above it met,

---

[18] See Jonathan Bate, *Shakespeare and Ovid* (Oxford: Clarendon Press, 1993), 185 and Thompson, 126-7.

> It looked from the bottome of the whoorlepoole up aloft
> As if it were from hell too heaven. (580-4)[19]

Translating from the same episode in *Metamorphoses* 11, Golding also writes: "The surges mounting up aloft did seeme too mate the skye, / And with theyr sprinckling for too wet the clowdes that hang on hye" (573-4). Jonathan Bate notes that Shakespeare may well have encountered this conventional image of the waves reaching the skies not in Ovid, but "in the rhetorical handbook of Susenbrotus, used in schools, where 'ad sidera fluctus' ('the waves to the stars') is illustrative of hyperbole" (185). Yet Bate also considers that Shakespeare's elaboration of this image in *Othello* 2.1 "is Ovidian in its specificity" (185) and its context.

Ovid's image of the waves reaching the skies, as Bate points out (185), punctuates his story of Ceyx and Alcyone, a husband and wife whose trials may be seen to anticipate the trials suffered by Othello and Desdemona. Ovid's lovers, like Shakespeare's, experience torments induced by separation, tempests at sea, portentous dreams, and, in the case of Alcyone and Othello, phantasmic delusion. In *Othello* 2.1.69-74, Shakespeare implicitly recalls Ovid's Alcyone in his description of Desdemona's apparent effect on the storm (Bate, 185). Desdemona calms "tempests themselves, high seas, and howling winds," which, "as having sense of beauty do omit / Their mortal natures, letting go safely by / The divine Desdemona" (2.1.68, 71-4); Alcyone's metamorphosed identity, that of the winged halcyon, is associated with seas that are "calme and still," "safe" for those who would "sayle . . . at will" (Golding, 11.859-60, cited by Bate).

In *Othello* 2.1, several Ovidian associations, including perhaps those established in *Heroides* 18 and 19 between Hero and Leander and Ceyx and Alcyone, open Shakespeare's presentation of Othello and Desdemona's love to meanings that are simultaneously poignant and forbidding. Ovid issues a double allusion to Ceyx and Alcyone in *Heroides* 18 and 19, as if he would underscore certain parallels between the two couples' experiences of love. In *Heroides* 18.77-82, as Leander describes the mysteriously calm, moonlit

---

[19] Citations from Golding are from *Shakespeare's Ovid, being Arthur Golding's translation of the Metamorphoses*, ed. W. H. D. Rouse (Carbondale: Southern Illinois Univ. Press, 1961).

night in which he first swam to Hero, he remembers that he heard the "sweet lament" of the halycons, "their hearts still true to beloved Ceyx":

> unda repercussae radiabat imagine lunae,
> et nitor in tacita nocte diurnus erat;
> nullaque vox usquam, nullum veniebat ad aures
> praeter dimotae corpore murmur aquae.
> Alcyones solae, memores Ceycis amati,
> nescio quid visae sunt mihi dulce queri.

In *Heroides* 19.191-204, Hero describes her surrender to what Ovid's reader knows is an ominous dream, a dream of wind-tossed waters and an abandoned corpse that replicates Alcyone's dream (*Metamorphoses* 11.651-76) of her drowned husband:

> Sed mihi, caeruleas quotiens obvertor ad undas,
> nescio quo pavidum frigore pectus hebet.
> nec minus hesternae confundor imagine noctis,
> quamvis est sacris illa piata meis.
> namque sub aurora, iam dormitante lucerna,
> somnia quo cerni tempore vera solent,
> stamina de digitis cecidere sopore remissis,
> collaque pulvino nostra ferenda dedi.
> hic ego ventosas nantem delphina per undas
> cernere non dubia sum mihi visa fide,
> quem postquam bibulis inlisit fluctus harenis,
> unda simul miserum vitaque deseruit.

Anticipating Shakespeare's lovers, Ovid's Hero and Leander and Ceyx and Alcyone confront not merely those storms that are raised by the elements, but also those raised by passion, fear, and doubt.

Beyond these subtle evocations of *Metamorphoses* 11 and *Heroides* 18 and 19, Othello's elaboration of the image of the waves reaching the stars also effects the first, and the most explicit, allusion to the *Tristia* within Shakespeare's play. *Tristia* 1.2.19-22 provides another description of the waves mounting to the heavens, and this description anticipates Othello's imaginings not merely in visual detail, but also in rhetorical patterns of formal elaboration and repetition:

me miserum, quanti montes volvuntur aquarum!
iam iam tacturos sidera summa putes.
quantae diducto subsidunt aequore valles!
iam iam tacturas Tartara nigra putes.

(Wretched me! what vast mountains of water heave themselves
aloft! Now, now, you think, they will touch the highest stars.
What mighty abysses settle beneath us as the flood yawns apart!
Now, now you think they will touch black Tartarus.)

Anticipating Othello, Ovid's speaker characterizes the storm-surge as something that forms mountains or hills. Like Othello, he uses words of violence and forced endeavor to convey the movement of and upon such waters (Ovid uses the verb "volvuntur"; Shakespeare the adjective "laboring"). Like Othello, Ovid's speaker also suggests that the sea's wild disequilibrium collapses the distinction between heaven and hell. Employing anaphora in the double repetition of "iam iam tacturos . . . iam iam tacturas," Ovid's passage sustains a sense of urgency, but, even more pertinent to Shakespeare's variation, a certain formality as well.

Recontextualized in Othello's speech in 2.1, the image of the world returned to chaos in *Tristia* 1.2 establishes what terrors Othello would endure if such terrors might be the prelude to love. The most elaborate recollection of the *Tristia* in Shakespeare's tragedy, this passage foregrounds, and lends resonance to, the briefer, more implicit allusions to the *Tristia* that adumbrate Othello's fatal meditation on the currents of the Pontic sea. Ironically, of course, this first recollection, of the world returned to primal chaos in *Tristia* 1.2, also anticipates Othello's portentous lamentation in 3.3.90-3: "Perdition catch my soul / But I do love thee; and when I love thee not, / Chaos is come again." In these words, as in the simile that will follow, Shakespeare, according to the most literal associations of "perdition," permits the language of loss to complicate and deepen that of damnation. Recalling the effects of the storm that initially parted the lovers as they sailed to Cyprus, Othello's reference to chaos in line 93 implies his new resolve to endure that storm raised by his own will rather than by nature: the storm that is the prelude to death rather than love.

Haunted by Ovid and Marlowe, Othello's extended simile in 3.3.453-62 is extraordinarily complex. The allusive dynamics of the simile display Shakespeare's learning, opening Othello's words to meanings that unsettle his intent to carry himself beyond emotional inconstancy or change through an insistent rhetoric of formal repetition.[20] Referencing Ovid's and Marlowe's Hellespont, Othello's declaration of murder is opened to a fleeting recollection of others' dark plights of love. For an instant, through a saturated reference, Othello's words are mournful rather than, or as well as, vengeful. For an instant, they anticipate the affiliation of love and death enacted in the close of Shakespeare's tragedy.

The University of the South

---

[20] Thomas M. Greene's description of allusion as a phenomenon that "immerses us . . . in the flow of literary history" and "plunges us . . . deeply into the currents and eddies of this continuous flow of energy" subtends my interpretation of the dynamics of Shakespeare's literary recollections in *Othello* 3.3; see *The Light in Troy: Imitation and Discovery in Renaissance Poetry* (New Haven: Yale Univ. Press, 1982), 53. Also relevant to my argument that Shakespeare's allusions open Othello's words to meanings that extend beyond Othello's conscious intent is Stephen Hinds's discussion of intuition and simultaneity in certain instances of layered allusion or intertextuality; see *Allusion and Intertext: Dynamics of appropriation in Roman Poetry* (Cambridge: Cambridge Univ. Press, 1998), 13-4 et passim.

The Discourse of Dilution in *2 Henry IV*

NICHOLAS CRAWFORD

THE mood that pervades the action—or inaction—of *Henry IV, Part Two* is that of an interregnum, one that exists in spirit if not in fact. While the stage swells with Falstaff's bantering rhetoric, King Henry tosses and turns in the royal bedchamber and Prince Hal does little more than idle in indecision. Yet in spite of its place as the play between momentous events, this curiously swollen center of the *Henriad* is central to the meaning of the whole series and to its conception of history. Catherine Belsey has argued that the *Henriad* begins with the issue of meaning itself in *Richard II* and ends with the issue of power in *Henry V*. In her account, *Richard II* dramatizes the uncertainties generated when the name and the thing (the king in name and the king as the powerful thing it purports to be) do not necessarily correspond, while *Henry V* questions, as it also affirms, the legitimacy of kingship: "Read from a postmodern perspective, they [the Lancastrian series] reveal marks of the struggle to fix meaning, and simultaneously of the excess which necessarily renders meaning unstable."[1] In other words, Belsey points out that the second tetralogy not only questions the monarchic order but also the fixity, authority, and legitimacy of language—not just the meaning of kingship but also the kingship of meaning.

The inability to fix meaning, particularly the meaning of kingship, leads in *2 Henry IV* to an excess of both discourse and delay. The King whose title the play bears does not even appear until the

[1] Catherine Belsey, "Making Histories Then and Now: Shakespeare from *Richard II* to *Henry V*," in *Uses of History: Marxism, Postmodernism and the Renaissance*, eds. Francis Barker et al (Manchester, England: Manchester Univ. Press, 1991), 32-3.

top of the third act. The protagonist Prince, in whose future the
fate of the country lies, dawdles in the wings until the second act
has almost wound down. In place of the monarchic machinations
we anticipate from the title, we find front and center Falstaff and
his various foils, who fritter time and toast the health of sickened
merriment. While the king ails with a mysterious disease, the people of the taverns and stews fester in afflictions better understood.
The land suffers from, as Falstaff announces, "This apoplexy . . . a
kind of lethargy . . . a sleeping in the blood" (1.2.114-6).[2] Things
cannot move forward but are rather stuck in an all pervasive "gravy,
gravy, gravy" that bogs and clogs the streams of social circulation
(1.2.165). A number of critics have remarked on how Falstaff
seems to embody this spirit of swollen stasis. Patricia Parker, in
particular, has argued persuasively that early modern thinking on
the rhetorical scheme of *copia* and its relation to *dilatio* ("the 'dilation of Christendom' . . . through the 'dilation of the Word'")
should be brought to bear on our reading of the *Henriad*.[3] *Dilatio's*
double sense of dilation and deferral appears to describe the groan-
ing corpulence and expansive garrulity of Falstaff and his relation to
Hal's delays.

Dilatio, however, and the more secular expression *copia* were
rhetorical schemes not generally intended either to produce laugh-
ter, or to typify the buffoonery of a Falstaff or to disperse focused
thought. On the contrary, the "full" style was a rhetorical ideal. As
Russ McDonald explains, during the Renaissance "The noun
'copia' was interchangeable with 'eloquence' because fullness or va-

---

[2] *Henry IV, Part 2*, eds. Barbara A. Mowat and Paul Werstine, The
New Folger Library Shakespeare (New York: Washington Square Press,
1999). All references to *2H4* are to this edition. Additionally, quotations
from all plays will be cited parenthetically in the text.

[3] Patricia Parker, *Literary Fat Ladies: Rhetoric, Gender, Property*
(New York: Methuen, 1987), 9. Parker also explains here how the Latin
dilato (for spreading out or dilation) and *dilatio* (with a sense closer to
delay) conflate in the hands of the Church fathers. In this paper, the double (almost Derridean) meaning will always be referred to as *dilatio*. See
also how this critic connects Falstaff to the important gender component
of her argument on *copia*, dilation, and the generation of the text. For a
discussion of Falstaff figured feminine, see also Valerie Traub, "Prince
Hal's Falstaff: Positioning Psychoanalysis, and the Female Reproductive
Body," *Shakespeare Quarterly* 40 (1989): 456-74.

riety of statement was considered a virtue in and of itself."[4] Writing on the virtues of *copia*, Erasmus names it the "style [that] speaks most full, and enriches its matter with as varied an ornamentation as possible, expanding the subject until nothing can be added to it."[5] *Henry IV, Part 2* vigorously explores the limits and veracity of the Erasmian credo by testing the point at which *dilatio* and *copia*, expansion and fullness, necessarily dilute and diffuse the matter of meaning rather than contribute to its construction and consolidation through elaboration. Additionally, as we have seen, at the center of *2 Henry IV*—and the *Henriad* in general—is the meaning of kingship. The pervasive metaphors of obstruction, stasis (sometimes in the form of repetition), and swelling serve to figure the threat of (or perhaps wish for) the dilution of monarchic political power.[6]

The very first lines of the play foreground the dilution of meaning and kingship by employing tropes of dilation and obstruction: "*Rumor.* Open your ears, for which of you will stop / The vent of hearing when loud Rumor speaks?" (1.1.1-2). The orifice of the ear is commanded to dilate unobstructed; however, when the "vent of hearing" is filled with rumor, meaning is diluted in a flood of lies. In this Induction, Rumor speaks falsely, claiming that Hotspur has actually slain Harry Monmouth. Thus Rumor undermines Hal's consolidation of power as successor to the king. Personified Rumor highlights the possibility that copious rhetoric and truth may at times be antithetical to one another, and that such verbal license may also undermine the meaning of monarchy. Following the dictates of Renaissance rhetoricians, copious rhetoric should sharpen meaning by elaboration, not dull it by pointless digressions and tedious repetition or misrepresent it through runaway rumors. The aim is to hold up the object of inquiry at all angles to better illuminate its full substance.

---

[4] Russ McDonald, *Shakespeare and the Arts of Language* (Oxford and New York: Oxford Univ. Press, 2000), 27.

[5] Quoted in Lee A. Sonnino, *A Handbook to Sixteenth-Century Rhetoric* (New York: Barnes & Noble, Inc., 1968), 216.

[6] Just as dilution of kingship gestures toward democratization, Nina Levine's economic model in "Extending Credit in the *Henry IV* Plays" seems to point toward the map of a future market economy. See *Shakespeare Quarterly* 51 (2000): 403-31.

But if we switch to a more liquid metaphor—one perhaps better
suited to alehouse locales and the dreamy fluidity of Henry's bedchamber scenes—we find that to speak of filling the basin of
thought to the rim is to imply diluting the concentration of the discursive object. In Falstaff and his belly we have, as C. L. Barber
puts it, "a symbol of the process of inflation and collapse of meaning," or a thinning of significance by means of rhetorical larding.[7]
The copiousness of Falstaff's discourse signals not a fullness of
thought but rather the expansion of thin wit and the dilution of
serious purpose. In this model of dilution by dilation, we always
find this double action: an increase in one sense and a corresponding decrease in another; put more formulaically, the concentration
of signification is inversely proportional to the volume of talk. Falstaff is in essence the personification of dilation as dilution; he is
increase and substance as puff and bluster, *copia* as concentration's
obverse.

Despite his massive solidity, Falstaff's first line in the play refers
to his liquidity, to the questionable health of his urine: "Sirrah, you
giant, what says the doctor to my water?" (1.2.1). As Doll
Tearsheet will later tell us, "There's a whole merchant's venture of
Bordeaux stuff in him" (2.4.64-5). That which makes Falstaff great
in girth dilutes and pollutes his constitution. Similarly, in his very
first appearance in the play, Prince Hal expresses his fear of precisely this threat to the health of his "greatness." It is as if nothing
could imperil his royalty more than to be plagued by a Falstaffian
pattern of alcoholic dilution:

> *Prince.* Doth it not show vilely in me to desire small beer?
> *Poins.* Why, a prince should not be so loosely studied as to re-
> member so weak a composition.
> *Prince.* . . . I do now remember the poor creature small beer. But
> indeed these humble considerations make me out of love with my
> greatness. (2.2.5-12)

What is liquid largesse for Falstaff is for Hal a dilution of princeli-
ness. And just two scenes later, Falstaff's humble beer-engendered

---

[7] C. L. Barber, *Shakespeare's Festive Comedy: A Study of Dramatic
Form and its Relation to Social Custom* (Princeton: Princeton Univ.
Press, 1959), 121.

urine figures even more explicitly as a transgressive jester's threat to the dignity of kingship:

> *Falstaff.* (singing) When Arthur first in court–
> (To *Will*) Empty the jordan.
> And was a worthy king– (2.4.33-5)

The grand narrative of English monarchy has been here reduced to a tavern tune, then further debased by the interruption from the fat pisser and his brimming pot of waste. And in the story of the play, Falstaff has delayed—if not directly interrupted—Hal's reformation and diluted his resolve. No one more than Hal is affected by Falstaffian discourse, no one more diluted in his purpose and his person, or in the meaning of his estate. Falstaff is "a mirror of human mutability in his use of words, as well as in his definition of them."[8] If he is then, as he says he is, "the cause that wit is in other men" (1.2.10), the wit that he causes serves to befuddle, to arrest the directionality of thought, to undermine meaning in general and thus subvert the meaning of kingship in particular. What Henry finds— and Hal later—most pernicious in Falstaff's influence is not his ability to delay and distract the royal purpose but to dilute with sack the royal resolve, to threaten to weaken the supposed kingly character of his companion prince by so saturating his life with merrymaking and jest that the concentration of his character is washed thin by a watery wit.

Dilatory rhetoric gone the way of the rhetoric of dilution is not only practiced by Falstaff and the other denizens of Eastcheap, it sets the dramatic mood and functions as the central trope of the play; for nothing characterizes *2 Henry IV* so much as the spirit of swelling stagnation, delay, stuck-in-a-rut iteration, a kind of incessant pooling that finds no egress; there is obstruction, dilation, and increase, but also—and necessarily so—dilution.

From a rhetorical point of view, the scheme that most strikingly illustrates this quality of obstruction and inflation is the frequently employed repetition of words or phrases known as *epizeuxis*. Iteration can be a mode of insistence and emphasis, but it can also be

---

[8] Jane Donawerth, *Shakespeare and the Sixteenth-Century Study of Language* (Urbana and Chicago: Univ. of Illinois Press, 1984), 18.

the hallmark of stasis, of the repetitive, a dilution of the original through rampant reproduction. Examples in the play abound:

> *Hostess.* . . . and I have borne and borne, and borne, and have been fubbed off, and fubbed off, and fubbed off . . . Do your offices, do your offices, . . . do me, do me, do me your offices. (2.1.32-41)

> *Shallow.* Come on, come on, come on. Give me your hand, sir, give me your hand, sir. (3.2.1-2)

> *Shallow.* Where's the roll? Where's the roll? Where's the roll? Let me see, let me see, let me see. So, so, so, so. so. So, so. (3.2.100-3)

> *Shallow.* Barren, barren, barren. (5.3.7)

> *Falstaff.* My womb, my womb, my womb. (4.3.22)

Renaissance rhetoricians suggest the use of *epizeuxis* to concentrate the impact and effect of the oration, to heighten the emotional tenor of the expression. Swiss rhetorician Joannes Susenbrotus defines the term as "When we repeat a word unnaturally in the full flow of utterance for the sake of greater vehemence," and he is echoed in 1577 by the English grammarian Henry Peachum, who writes, "A word is repeated, for the greater vehemency."[9] In the later tragedies, Shakespeare uses this technique as recommended "to suggest great intensity of feeling: as in Lear's 'Howl, howl, howl, howl!'"[10] But Shakespeare is up to something else in his use of *epizeuxis* in *2 Henry IV.* [11]

---

[9] Quoted in Sonnino, 174-5.

[10] Katie Wales, "An A-Z of Rhetorical Terms," in *Reading Shakespeare's Dramatic Language: A Guide*, eds. Sylvia Adamson et al. (London: The Arden Shakespeare, 2001), 271-301.

[11] See Adrian Pilkington, *Poetic Effects: A Relevance Theory Perspective* (Amsterdam: John Benjamins Publishing Company, 2000), 125, for discussion of how "a range of stylistic effects . . . may be offered by . . . *epizeuxis*." Similarly, Brian A. Vickers, *In Defense of Rhetoric* (Oxford: Clarendon Press, 1988), 338, offers an example from Shakespeare where the effect of *epizeuxis* is the opposite of heightened emotion: "the Nurse's erroneously premature lament for the death of Juliet: O woe! O woeful,

The effect then of these repetitions is not to concentrate or intensify the meaning of the utterance but rather to diffuse and dilute its power. Speech becomes cheaper and cheaper in Eastcheap—prose for the people and poetry for potentates. The concentration of political power in the court is matched by the concentration of meaning in the poetic language spoken there. By contrast, the sprawling and repetitive prose of the pubs reflects a dilution of both power and meaning. Through bluster and repetition, words are sapped of their particular force. This general diffusion and dilution rather than dilation (in the rhetorical sense) drains the play and its characters of directional energy. Here *copia*, in the sense of full expression, gives way to the sense of copying, another word of which *copia* is the Latin root. Copious copying is not full expression but redundancy that dilutes and decreases the power of the original. Shallow's repetitions do not render him more intense but rather more diffuse, spread thin, shallow, in fact. The incessant reiterations almost to the point of a stutter by Falstaff, Mistress Quickly, and especially Shallow are also vocal demonstrations of these characters' inability—like Prince Hal's—to proceed forward. They are stuck, stuck on a word, stuck on a phrase, stuck between times, between reigns, just as Prince Hal is stuck between youth and maturity, between the tavern and the throne, between one who is unruly and one who rules. Their energy and verbosity seem largely wasted, as does their time.[12] Falstaff complains, "I were better to be eaten to death with a rust than to be scoured to nothing with perpetual motion" (1.2.224-5). But so he is 'scoured' instead with pointless repetition, the linguistic analogue of perpetual motion.

Certainly repetition at the level of word and phrase is part of a much grander scheme of doubling and repeating, circling and stagnating. The whole play, as a number of critics have observed, repeats *1 Henry IV* to a degree, but also seems a darker shadow of its predecessor: "*2 Henry IV* is a still more disillusioning play than Part One: it promises to repeat the design of the first play but then

---

woeful, woeful day! . . . Since the grief is unfounded, those lines are obviously meant to be ridiculous."

[12] As Maurice Hunt formulates the situation, "Hal projects the time that he wastes with Falstaff onto the fat knight, converting his companion into a figure of 'wasted time.'" See "Time and Timelessness in *Henry IV*," *Explorations in Renaissance Culture* 10 (1984): 59.

frustrates our expectation" with its alternating tavern and court scenes, which now appear less fresh than in their original incarnations.[13] The elaborate punning on Old Double and his death resonates with the death of the play's doubling, the moment when the drama's singularity of direction finally does take shape in the rejection of Falstaff and the transformation of Hal. Nevertheless, through most of the play the copious copying from *1 Henry IV* expands the meaning of each scene by tacit reference to similar previous ones, while at the same time diluting the concentrated specificity of context through the repetition of similar words and images. Patricia Parker shrewdly seizes on the connections and implications of this complex doubling:

> In the *second* part of *Henry IV* . . . iteration as the mechanical reproduction of the 'cuckoospell' [Puttenham's nickname for *epizeuxis*] or doublet is repeatedly linked with seconding, copying, and representing . . . its 'Harry Harry'—the very formula of royal succession—becomes yet one more of the play's incessant iterations of the cuckoo song or verbal doublet.[14]

On the one hand such doubling and copying is *copia*, a kind of increase and elaboration, yet it is also, as I have argued, a form of dilution, a subversion of the original. To double the king is not to double kingship but rather to cut by half the concentration of power. Just as Shallow's repetitive speech serves only to highlight his ineffectuality and the unreliability of his discourse, the presence of two Harrys makes each seem less than king. We see this anxiety toward (or desire for) kingly reproduction and the attendant dilution of power engaged at the end *Henry IV, Part I* when the soldiers on the battlefield disguise themselves as the king in order to make him difficult to identify and kill. The situation of having, in effect, two kings (one a sickened, ineffectual Henry and the other an impetuous, uncertain prospect for succession) is tantamount to

---

[13] David Bevington, "Introduction," in *Henry the Fourth Parts I and II: Critical Essays*, ed. David Bevington (New York: Garland Publishing Co., 1986), 19.

[14] Patricia Parker, *Shakespeare from the Margins: Language, Culture, Context* (Chicago & London: Univ. of Chicago Press, 1996), 161.

having half a king. The Henrys are literally doubled but metaphorically halved. The paradox of increase as a figure of dilution is brought into high relief when applied to kingship. The throne is dependent upon the idea of a unique, solo ruler. More soldiers make for a more powerful army, but more kings make for a weaker state.

The image of a battlefield full of counterfeit kings at the end of *1 Henry IV* reminds one of Walter Benjamin's analysis of "The Work of Art in the Age of Mechanical Reproduction," a critique aimed at a supposedly purely modern phenomenon. As Benjamin warns, "the presence of the original is the prerequisite to the concept of authenticity."[15] Even by the sixteenth century, the printing press may have already changed all that in the early modern world. We see Benjamin's description of a modern *angoisse* toward the loss of the unique art object prefigured in the early portions of the second tetralogy's treatment of kingship. Just as the availability of innumerable posters of the Mona Lisa threatens to render the authenticity of the original painting less sacrosanct, the topos of multiple monarchs in the *Henriad* undermines the crown's status as the unique locus of legitimate power. There is another side, however, to the anxiety produced by such disruptions of accepted notions of originality and to the expansion of the location of legitimate power. Concurrent with society's worry that power and meaning have been destabilized comes a populist glee at gaining access, a joy in disposing of the status given to a solitary source of signification and authority. Everyone can have a piece of the Mona Lisa; everyone can be, in part, the king of England. Meaning and power are disseminated and diluted but also democratized. And the Henry plays seem to register this double movement as cause for both concern and celebration.

In *Henry V*, power is of course finally and unequivocally consolidated, but this play too is not without ambiguities. Should we, as Fluellen and Gower debate, liken Henry V to "Alexander the Great" or rather to "Alexander the Pig?" (4.7.12-3).[16] As Norman

---

[15] Walter Benjamin, *Illuminations* (1936), trans. Harry Zohn (New York: Harcourt, Brace & World, Inc., 1968), 222.

[16] *Henry V*, eds. Barbara A. Mowat and Paul Werstine, The New Folger Library Shakespeare (New York: Washington Square Press, 1995). All references to the play are from this edition.

Rabkin explains, the play supports both readings, as it is much like the animal drawings of gestaltists that seem to depict, for example, either a rabbit or a duck, depending upon how they are viewed. Thus Rabkin insists that the play is neither "rabbit" nor "duck" but "could scarcely have been anything but a rabbit-duck."[17] At any given time, we can see only one "animal" or the other, but both are there. It is as if the picture that Shakespeare gives us in *Henry V*—like the conjurer's trick—actually contains both images, but the viewer's line of sight and the conjurer's sleight of hand will determine which one will emerge temporarily predominant. If by complicating Hal's apparent glorification in *Henry V* Shakespeare is registering a measure of skepticism toward monarchic entitlement, or at least toward Hal's martial ambitions, he is perhaps embedding that same message in the second Henry play by means of protraction and delay.

We should then consider that the static swelling of *2 Henry IV* may not simply be action obstructed but a different *kind* of action, a sort of "loiterature," as Ross Chambers terms a vein of meandering modern letters—or the "literature of hanging out."[18] Chambers asks, "Does loiterature just loiter? Or does it loiter with intent? And if the latter, is that the intent—to register a certain withholding of assent not by saying so but through dilatory discursive gesturing."?[19] By delaying the appearance and significant actions of both the king and the prince, and by filling the play with the sorry boasts and touching troubles of the disaffected, disenfranchised, and dipsomaniacal Shakespeare seems this time to be tilting the picture in such a way as to compel us to see the relatively powerless more clearly at first. To fill the stage with Falstaff is to remind the audience not only that life is large but that the empty force of alehouse rhetoric has a kind of power in its harmless license, that it is perhaps no less ridiculous than the small-mindedness of kingly concerns, constrained as they are by the tightly-wrought liberties of the crown's speech and the dire consequences it can engender. Falstaff has the freedom and the power to destabilize discourse precisely

---

[17] Norman Rabkin, "Rabbits, Ducks, and *Henry V*," *Shakespeare Quarterly* 28 (1977): 279-96, 280.

[18] Ross Chambers, *Loiterature* (Lincoln & London: Univ. of Nebraska Press, 1999), 291.

[19] Ibid.

because, apart from his marginal recruiting endeavors, he can claim he speaks for himself and not the state.

Conversely, Hal, the Lord Chief Justice, and all those closely associated with the court have no such freedom. The Chief Justice, as representative of Law and King, recognizes Falstaff as his official counterpart, as the representative of the misrule of meaning. Carrying out his duties as the keeper of the fixity and stability of meaning, the Chief Justice warns Falstaff that "not a confident brow, nor the throng of words that come with such more than impudent sauciness from you, can thrust me from a level consideration" (2.1.116-9). Ultimately, Hal lauds the Chief Justice for displaying a similar immovable severity in his own case. As part of Hal's migration from the flux of Falstaffian freedoms to the fixity of rule, he not only pardons but praises the Chief Justice's early actions against him, when the Justice did "rate, rebuke, and roughly send to prison / Th'immediate heir of England" (5.2.71-2). The transformation of Hal from borderline wastrel to resolute ruler coincides with a recognition that locates the force, stability, and regulated flow of meaning in the crown itself, in the oratorical office of the king rather than in the supposed divine right that his father lacks and that his father's death seems to mock. Harry, gone to die in the Jerusalem chamber, perishes as a still uneasy usurper of the crown, and does so in a place indelibly yet ironically linked to the King of Kings and hence to the notion of monarchic divine right, as well as to the origin of the Word, to the source of belief in the ultimately absolute and unchanging nature of meaning. In turn, Prince Hal vows:

> To frustrate prophecies, and to raze out
> Rotten opinion, who hath writ me down
> After my seeming. The tide of blood in me
> Hath proudly flowed in vanity till now.
> Now doth it turn and ebb back to the sea,
> Where it shall mingle with the state of floods
> And flow henceforth in formal majesty. (5.2.127-32)

In essence, Hal promises to rewrite the rumored story of his only seeming prosaic nature and link his lot to the poetic majesty of state. These images, reflective of an identity negotiated between self and state, are figured liquid and linked to a washing away, a dilution of "Rotten opinion," which will now be reinscribed in a language of concentrated "formal majesty." And indeed, with Falstaff in Eastcheap, the Prince has spoken a careless prose. In his declarations of his intent to rule, however, and in the court with his father, and finally now with the Chief Justice, Hal speaks only verse, elegant and modulated. When Hal apologizes to his father for donning the crown, he explains that he "spake unto this crown as having sense" (4.3.313). What Hal comes to understand when he finally in effect becomes the crown is that the crown does not hear, is not a recipient of meaning but rather its source. To wear the crown and enjoy its bully pulpit is to "act out the rhetoricians' fantasy of conquest and rule through language," but it is also, as Wayne Rebhorn notes, to engage in "the rhetorical performance of rule [which] actually makes the monarch the 'subject' of his subjects—and of his performance itself."[20] Thus the king is both the ultimate ruler and rhetor as well as the most constructed—and hence most constrained—of early modern subjects.

Though Hal does eventually adopt the formal flow to which he alludes, the role of reasoned ruler, advancing by diction that is purposeful and precise, he lingers for an intriguingly long time in the role of unreliable rascal, choosing to inhabit the static realm of the between, of "loiterature," where meaning is messy and the noisy narrative goes nowhere. Characterized by aimless, diluted action and time distended, we note that "Loiterature distracts attention from what it's up to, and in that it's a bit like the street conjurer whose patter diverts us from what's really going on. But then, maybe nothing much *is* going on after all."[21] Compare this to Stephen Greenblatt's famous analysis of the *Henriad* in "Invisible Bullets," in which he finds that *Henry IV, Part Two* retroactively makes the 'balance' of *1 Henry IV*

> on closer inspection seem like radical instability tricked
> out as moral or aesthetic order; what appeared as clarity
> may seem now like the conjurer's trick concealing confu-

---

[20] Wayne A. Rebhorn, *The Emperor of Men's Minds: Literature and the Renaissance Discourse of Rhetoric* (Ithaca & London: Cornell Univ. Press, 1995), 78-9.

[21] Chambers, 9.

sion in order to buy time and stave off the collapse of an illusion.[22]

And indeed, *Part Two* begins to seem more and more like "loiterature," as Falstaff and Hal—and we might even be duped into including Shakespeare here as well—behave as though there is all the time in the world. We sense, however, that it is all a conjuring trick, that time is and always has been running out, and that we, like Hal, are being distracted from this fact by the illusion of stasis. The conjurer's "trick of loiterly narrative is . . . that the alleged story becomes all middle."[23] Beginnings and endings are revealed to be the illusions they are. Life, like Falstaff, is all middle. And what is the second Henry play if not all middle?

Henry IV, Part 2 comes, of course, between *Henry IV, Part 1* and *Henry V*, but more than that it is the play of the middle, the play of the between. More than marking once again the end of one reign and the beginning of another, *Henry IV, Part 2* paints the space between kingships. Whereas Bolingbroke signaled his rise to power with the dynamic usurpation of Richard's throne, Prince Hal succeeds to the crown through a process of seemingly static inevitability, through a persistent bloating and festering of immovable circumstance that must eventually cede to rupturing. The mediary quality of the drama develops not only through the various tropes of dilation and schemes of repetition we have seen, it informs the dilution of meaning in the two most celebrated scenes in the play. Prince Hal's donning of his father's crown and the rejection of Falstaff powerfully demonstrate how central (and the pun is intended) the quality of being betwixt and between is to an understanding of not only the structure and language of *Henry IV, Part 2* but the whole tetralogy. These two scenes also demonstrate the connection between repetition and dilution. The moments that are reiterations or adumbrations of previous scenes add to meaning in one sense and dilute it in another.

In King Harry's first appearance, smack in the middle of the play, we find him between wakefulness and sleep. He dreams of

---

[22] Stephen Greenblatt, *Shakespearean Negotiations: The Circulation of Social Energy in Renaissance England* (Berkeley: Univ. of California Press, 1988), 47.

[23] Chambers, 21.

sleep and is awake as if dreaming. This serves as a proleptic image for Prince Hal's entrance to the king's bedchamber in the fourth act. With the eerie logic of fantasy and dream, Hal elects to place the crown upon his own head, thus rendering himself more than prince but still less than king. He is playing at being king, just as earlier in the drama he has played at being a tavern joker by donning a jerkin and waiting on Falstaff. The moment Hal exits the bedchamber, his father pops awake—indicating perhaps that he was, as in the earlier scene, still between wake and sleep—and demands to know the whereabouts of his crown. Hal is between the court and the tavern, between playacting and plain action, between prince and king, between the dream of kingship and the reality of his princely dereliction in Eastcheap.

When Hal later rejects Falstaff, he figures the fat knight as a dream image, and in rejecting him he rejects his own self-described state between reality and dreams, between the reality of his princely purpose and the dream of diversion in which he claims he has only partly engaged as a kind of actor. From early in *Henry IV, Part 1*, Hal lets us know that when he is with Falstaff at the Boar's Head Tavern he is not entirely himself, that he is between who he really is (and like the sun will be "when he please again to be himself") and the part he has been seduced to play as Falstaff's sidekick (1.2.193).[24] And who is John Falstaff? Surely not Sir John Oldcastle, or so we are told in the Epilogue. While playgoers no doubt see a resemblance between the stage character and the real life nobleman, they still appreciate Falstaff as something between a pure invention and the notorious knight that the Epilogue purports he is not.

This sense of perpetual vacillation between incipient identities finds its source in the second tetralogy's interplay of scenes, in both the additive and dispersive result of their accumulation. Stephen Greenblatt has demonstrated, for example, that Falstaff's proclamation that "The undeserver may sleep when the man of action is call'd on" (2.4.385) is not only hot air but is a kind of "anticipatory, or proleptic, parody" of the king's coming soliloquy on his insomnia.[25] If we may accept Greenblatt's contention that the anticipatory aspect of scenes later adumbrated is "a major structural principle of

---

[24] *Henry IV, Part I*, ed. Claire McEachern, *The Pelican Shakespeare* (New York: Penguin, 2000). All references are to this edition.
[25] Greenblatt, 54-5.

Shakespeare's play," we might then see that Henry's insomnia scene anticipates and lends a certain contrapuntal irony to Hal's rejection of Falstaff.[26] Where Bolingbroke has wanted nothing so much as sleep and has deemed the worries of kingship the great impediment to slumber, the new king despises sleep and sees its dreams as his downfall: "I have long dreamt of such a kind of man, / So surfeit-swelled, so old, and so profane; / But being awaked, I do despise my dream" (*2H4* 5.5.49-51). In fact, both Harry and Hal see themselves somewhere between reality and dreams, but Harry yearns for sleep and Hal wills himself fully awake. The irony is that Harry sees inhabiting the space between wakefulness and dreams as an unfortunate burden of kingship, whereas Hal views his situation of being stuck between a kingly reality and a dream of degeneration as a burden to be cast off, to be thrust upon Falstaff. Shakespeare has prepared us for this moment since Hal's "Redeeming time" speech early in the first Henry play, when the prince informs us that he "Shall show more goodly and attract more eyes / Than that which hath no foil to set it off" (1.2.207-8). Put otherwise, he will look better in the future if he looks as bad as Falstaff now. Again, these scenes are adumbrations, repetitions, whose meaning retrospectively dilutes the singularity of meaning they held in previous scenes while simultaneously adding significance to the scene we presently witness. In other words, we have both *dilatio* and dilution, both *copia* as increase and *copia* as copy, both a furthering of fullness and a subversion or dilution and diminishment of the original.

Hal's rejection of Falstaff is then also a rejection of liminality and "loiterature," of stasis and dilution, of the prolix and purposeless story that has no referent in action. It is a repudiation of history on hold. As Patricia Parker points out, the Latin *delatare* is related to *dilatio* and can imply not only dilation and delay but accusation: "In *Othello*, the coincidence of dilation with delation—of amplification with accusation—comes something closer to what Derrida calls the demand for narrative as the power of the police."[27] We see this dynamic at work in *2 Henry 4* where, after so much dilation and delay, we come to the newly enforcement-oriented Hal, who as

---

[26] Ibid.

[27] Patricia Parker, "Shakespeare and Rhetoric: 'dilation' and 'delation' in *Othello*," in *Shakespeare and the Question of Theory*, eds. Patricia Parker and Geoffrey Hartman (New York: Methuen, 1985), 69.

king accuses Falstaff of being the cause of those delays and demands that we get on with the story of history that he will now
make.

And yet that history, like history before it, will be diluted by
Rumor, by figures such as Shallow, who will be full of stories. As
Falstaff reminds us, "how subject we old men are to this vice of lying. This same starved justice hath done nothing but prate . . . and
every third word a lie" (*2H4* 3.2.313-8). History is not what happens but what is said about what happens. Some of what is said
must be true, but much of it is not. While Rumor is the repetitious
producer of rampant untruths, even accurate individual accounts are
inadvertently biased and limited. The truth of history is to be found
then in the spaces between the various recordings of the past.[28] The
old cliché that history is written by the winners is inscribed into the
Henriad in Hal's unanswerable account and rejection of his and
Falstaff's friendship, while at the same time such inscriptions are
resisted and partially erased by the chatter of Eastcheap, the verbal
variegations which dilute the concentration of voices chosen for
historical chronicling. The authorized account of the crown is not
able to drown out entirely the marginal voices of the tavern. Hal
may make history in France, but first he makes up the history of his
and Falstaff's relationship. And while it is his version that endures
most easily, other accounts cannot be entirely suppressed. The
meaning of the king is thus bound up with the fact that by virtue of
his power he is also the king of meaning. But Shakespeare shows us
in the middle of the *Henriad* that meaning and history are ultimately inseparable and uncontainable. They exist only in the *copia*,
dilatio, and dilution of recounted narratives—and in the silence of
the multitude.

University of North Carolina at Greensboro

---

[28] D. M. Bergeron argues that Shakespeare's characters "make unlikely
the possibility that a single 'historical truth' can be attained." In particular,
he examines Falstaff's role in making history by incorporating fiction. See
"Shakespeare Makes History: *2 Henry IV*," *SEL: Studies in English Literature* 31 (1991): 231-46.

John Donne and "All the World"

GRAHAM ROEBUCK

ERY little is said about Donne and the theatre by his con-
temporaries. Of this little by far the most intriguing is the
well-known observation of Sir Richard Baker (1568-1645)
that Donne was "a great frequenter of Playes." Consequently, modern scholarship and criticism have sometimes felt prompted to assert that Donne was so intimately familiar with the popular theatre
of the day that explication and criticism of his poetry should proceed with the theatre as a principal context. It has also been
thought, on the other hand, that Baker's remark is valuable principally as a biographical referent, a report on an aspect of Donne's
youthful activity that should not be extrapolated into a literary-
interpretive nostrum. This critical caution, taken a stage further,
yields the view that to give any significant weight to Baker's remark
is actually misleading in view of the coolness, even hostility, of
Donne to the popular theatre, evidenced by the meager references
in his poetry to the stage, and the evident antagonism of his references to it in his sermons.

This essay first discusses, in broad terms, the significance of this
range of reaction to the question of Donne's attitude to the popular
theatre of the day. It then suggests a context for examination of one
of the Holy Sonnets—"This is my playes last scene"—in connection with part of Act II, scene 4 of *Henry IV, Part 1*.

The relevant passage in Baker's *A Chronicle of the Kings of
England* is located by the Index entry, "Doctor *Donne*, and his
commendation." Although literary scholars seldom rhapsodize over
chronicles, even less so over their indexes, in its own small way this

entry is remarkable, notwithstanding the anonymity of its author:[1] only national events and great kings are afforded their own entries. Donne is the exception. Compare this with Shakespeare, entered as "*William Shakespeare*, an excellent writer of Comedies," who is found clustered with Sherburne Castle and Abbey in a long list under the heading "Sheep—the greatest rot that ever was known, & continued 25 years." By contrast, Donne is heralded in a side note, "Two eminent Wits, Dr. Dunne, and Sir Henry Wotton." The passage reads:

> And here I desire the Readers leave to remember two of my own, old acquaintants, the one was Mr. *John Dunne*, who leaving *Oxford*, lived at the *Innes of Court*, not dissolute, but very neat; a great Visiter of Ladies, a great frequenter of Playes, a great Writer of conceited Verses; untill such time as King *James* taking notice of the pregnancy of his Wit, was a means that he betook him to the study of Divinity, and thereupon proceeding Doctor, was made Dean of *Pauls*; and became so rare a Preacher, that he was not onely commended, but even admired by all that heard him.[2]

It is no surprise that Baker chooses to emphasize Donne's role as preacher, in the approved manner—Baker knew his hierarchies— but what is his tone in the trilogy of greats: "great Visiter of Ladies . . . great frequenter of Playes . . . great Writer of conceited Verses"? Given his denial that the young Donne was a rake—"not dissolute, but very neat"[3]—we should not rush to assume Baker intends disapprobation of his old friend, notwithstanding the Jack Donne / Doctor Donne paradigm that seems to inform the passage. Perhaps we can gather a fuller sense of his disposition toward popular theater from his remarks on Shakespeare that conclude his list of "Men

---

[1] Anonymous, if Baker did not create his own index.

[2] *A Chronicle of the Kings of England* (London, 1643), Division 4, p. 156.

[3] OED gives no unequivocal, precise seventeenth-century sense for either word. "Dissolute" ranges from sense of un-(dis)connected, as in joints, etc., to the modern sense of a kind of moral depravity; "neat" from undiluted, unpolluted to clear, shining.

of note in her [i.e., Elizabeth's] Time." Baker concludes his account of the careers of statesmen, soldiers, sailors, divines and scholars:

> After such men [learned divines, such as Jewell and Hooker], it might be thought ridiculous to speak of Stage Players; but seeing excellency in the meanest things deserves remembring, and *Boscius* [*sic*, corrected to *Roscius* in *Errata*] the Comedian is recorded in History with such commendation, it may·be allowed us to do the like with some of our Nation.

He praises Burbage ["Bourbidge"] & Alleyn ["Allen"]—"no age must ever look to see the like"—and Tarleton, who "never had his match, never will have." These sound like the sentiments of a fan of the theater, whose enthusiasm is tempered by his sense of writing, beneath his dignity, of ridiculous things. Then he proceeds to "Writers of Playes, and such as had been Players themselves, *William Shakespeare*, and *Benjamin Johnson*, [who] have specially left their Names recommended to posterity."[4]

So much for Baker. He leaves us with a question: could his Oxford classmate have been similarly ambivalent about theater, admiration striving with a sense of shame at the ridiculous? Some scholars, as I have suggested, see Donne and popular theater engaged in a fruitful, symbiotic relationship. This view is well exemplified in the seminal work—lately neglected—of Patrick Cruttwell, *The Shakespearean Moment and its Place in the Poetry of the 17th Century*. As a work of intellectual history it seeks to explicate those moments at which currents of thought came together to create the unique circumstances of artistic creativity. The most "vital" meeting-ground, Cruttwell writes, "was the theatre."

> This is the basis of what is dramatic in Donne: a deep and lively experience of the theatre in the years when the English drama was on the edge of its greatest moment—years when it meant more, to men of more than

---

[4] *Chronicle*, Division 4, p. 120. Baker also wrote *Theatrum Redivivum, or the Theatre Vindicated* in answer to Prynne's *Histrio-Mastix*. It appeared posthumously, 1662; later reprinted as *Theatrum Triumphans*, 1670.

usual sensibility and intellect, than ever before or since. The gulf between highbrow and lowbrow, courtly and popular, was beginning to close; for Donne as for Shakespeare from the 1600's, there was no gulf. The experience of the popular theatre could be yielded to, by a man as intellectual and as learned as Donne, with none of the polite and classical shudders which afflicted and inhibited the Sidneys and the Halls; and because it could be thus freely yielded to, it could in turn yield something of the greatest value, could be decisive in the moulding of Donne's creation.[5]

As an instance of how "natural" the metaphor of the theatre was to Donne, Cruttwell cites the Holy Sonnet, "This is my Playes last scene"(42). Yet, neither in this instance, the most clear-cut evocation of the theatrical stage in Donne's poems, nor in any other Donne poem, does Cruttwell argue for a specific theatrical experience, either of a Shakespearian play or of any other playwright of the period. Instead, Cruttwell bases his argument on the assertion that Donne's poems "abound in proofs" that Donne was a "great frequenter of Playes."

Yet the seeming absence of specific reference remains puzzling. Even Donne's laudatory Latin poem on *Volpone*, addressed to "*Amicissimo, et meritissimo BEN. JONSON*," makes no mention of stage performance. Donne employs his latinity here as his tribute to Jonson's own erudition and thus it duly appears in the front matter of the 1607 quarto of the play, and again in Jonson's 1616 *Works*. Donne need never have seen a performance to have penned the sentiments expressed in the poem—indeed, he studiously avoids any hint that *Volpone* might be a stage play.

It is not Cruttwell's purpose to establish that kind of connection between Donne and the theater; rather he is concerned to evoke a milieu comprised of connections and friendships in the circles of writers and their aristocratic patrons, men of "more than usual sensibility and intellect," as he puts it. It is generously drawn. Even so, and perhaps because the picture is so engaging, the paucity of direct

---

[5] *The Shakespearean Moment and its Place in the Poetry of the 17th Century* (New York: Random House, 1960), pp. 41-2.

theater references in Donne's poems prompts engagement with the question why that is the case.

Cruttwell was answered by Victor Harris who noted "Donne's coolness, even his antipathy, toward the theatre nearly every time he mentions it," which prompts Harris to hold "the contrary position that Donne rejects the theater, both public and private, and that he was never truly at home there even in his youth."[6] It should be added that at the center of Harris's position is his rejection of the "history of ideas" hypothesis—its progenitor T. S. Eliot—that the literary career of Donne is the glorious flowering of his "unified sensibility." Cruttwell's book nails its colors to the mast in celebrating men of "unusual sensibility." There is no point here revisiting this very well-traveled region, but rather next to consider what, if anything, more we know about Donne and the popular stage.

Harris reviews much of the relevant evidence: that John Heywood, Donne's grandfather, wrote interludes; that Jasper Heywood, his uncle, translated Senecan tragedies; the reference to Donne and others at the Mitre in the company of Inigo Jones in a pseudonymous 1612 poem; the 1615 letter of Coryate to the "Sireniacal Gentlemen," supposedly meeting at the Mermaid; Donne's role as Master of the Revels at Lincoln's Inn; and the later connection with Edward Alleyn, who became Donne's son-in-law. Of course, none of this necessarily adds up to anything substantial.

Harris weighs the value of the references to theatrical texts and events, almost all well-known, in Donne's work. There are references to *Tamburlaine*—one in "The Calme," the other in a letter to Lady Bedford with which Donne dramatizes to her his current sickness, as ominous as "Tamerlins last dayes black ensignes whose threatenings none escaped." John Hayward, in his edition of Donne, takes this to "suggest that at one time Donne did frequent the theatre," though he remarks the very few references to drama in Donne.[7] From these and other references to *Sermons*, *Satyres*, principally I, III & IV, the verse letter to "Sir Edward Herbert at Julyers," and one to Wotton—"Here's no more news . . .," several

---

[6] "John Donne and the Theatre," *PQ* (1962), 257-269.

[7] John Donne, Dean of St. Paul's, *Complete Poetry and Selected Prose*, revised ed. (London: Nonesuch, 1967), p. 787.

Elegies, several *Songs and Sonnets*, *Pseudo-Martyr* and *Ignatius his Conclave*, in which he remarks on its five-part "play of sorts," Harris arrives at the opinion that although Donne does "show some inclination towards dramatic idiom, some personal ties with people of the theatre and some indulgence toward show and spectacle," there is, whether early or late in his career, little evidence of "serious taste for the theatre, much less any commitment to it" (261). This is notably a much cooler appraisal of similar evidence that led Molly Mahood to the conclusion, with special reference to Marlowe, that Donne alludes with "easy familiarity in his letters to theatrical affairs."[8]

Harris's argument develops into the more forceful and more critically interesting position, energized by his rejection of Eliot's thesis, that "Donne's sensibility does not extend to the theatre . . . he is even contemptuous of everything connected with it—plays, playwrights, actors, playgoers, the theatre as art or as imitation, as a way of life or of looking at life" (262). Now here is a critical thrust worthy of some attention. Although there have been other contributions to our knowledge of Donne and the theater since the era of Cruttwell and Harris, I am not aware of any fully-fledged response to Harris's view. The remainder of this paper—itself not a fully-fledged response—attempts to suggest an instance of Donne's reaction to the stage in his verse.

Among the post-Harris claims of further echoes of the theater in Donne's writing is that made by Edward Le Comte concerning the letter beginning "I am no great voyager . . . " in which Donne quotes the Earl of Arundel's remark on the art of reading, adding, "I am so far from following his counsel as he was from Petruccio's." Le Comte explicates it in the following way: "What we have here is Donne's only reference to Shakespeare. He had seen *The Taming of the Shrew* (not printed until the 1623 Folio). It was notorious that Arundel was dominated by his wife."[9] Likewise, Gardner heard Shakespearian echoes in Donne's Elegy "On his Mistress." The lines

---

[8] *Poetry and Humanism* (London: Cape, 1950) p. 89.
[9] *Grace to a Witty Sinner* (NY: Walker & Co., 1965), p. 255.

> nor in bed fright thy Nurse
> With midnight startings, crying out, oh, oh
> Nurse, ô my love is slaine, I sawe him goe
> O'er the white Alpes alone; I saw him I,
> Assail'd, fight, taken, stabb'd, bleed, fall, and die. (49-54)

make it difficult for her "to parallel outside the drama the intensity of this valediction and not to connect its opening adjuration with the sense of fate that hangs over Shakespeare's lovers cruelly parted."[10]

Although such recovered echoes of Shakespeare in Donne add weight to the view that Donne was familiar with the popular theatre, they don't answer Harris's argument concerning Donne's distaste for the stage. But, on the other hand, neither does Harris strengthen his argument when he seeks to convert Donne's expressions of *contemptus mundi*—in, for example, *The Second Anniversary*—into contempt for the stage. Donne's line, "Shee, to whom all this world was but a stage" (l. 67), is an instance of Donne's using what Harris acknowledges to be "a common image which often implies just this sort of contempt for the world " (266). Because it is such a popular metaphor, with its application to all humankind and human activity, it is implausible that Donne expresses thereby his attitude to the contemporary theatre. "All the World's a Stage" is, of course, one of Shakespeare's most versatile metaphors. Jacques's anatomizing speech in *As You Like It* comes first to mind, along with Lear's "This great stage of fools." But it is by no means Shakespeare's exclusive property, and cannot reasonably be taken to signify his attitude to the theater any more than Donne's use of the metaphor signifies his attitude.

Harris rounds out his argument by aligning Donne with classical and patristic condemnations of the "deadly contagion" of theatre (Augustine). On this view, Donne becomes a didactic moralist, as if he somehow lacked the poet's recourse to the various voices of his personae. Harris's formula—"In poem after poem he [Donne] shows, further, his low regard for actors . . ."(263)—depends on

---

[10] *John Donne: The Elegies and the Songs and Sonnets* (Oxford: Clarendon Press, 1965), p. 140. See also H.M. Richmond, "Donne's Master: the Young Shakespeare," *Criticism* 15 (1973), 126-44.

reading the poems, and the *Satyres* in particular, as statements of viewpoint. Donne is not singularly anti-theater, as Harris implies, when Donne writes of "ideot actors" (*Satyre II*) and idle-minded spectators. Think of York's account in *Richard II* of the entry of the humiliated, deposed king into London:

> As in a theatre the eyes of men,
> After a well-grac'd actor leaves the stage,
> Are idly bent on him that enters next,
> Thinking his prattle to be tedious . . . (V.ii.23 ff)

Here the energy of the metaphor issues from amusement at our capacity to suspend disbelief conditionally for the "well-grac'd actor." It is about the subtle commerce between stage and audience: about illusions of reality. Likewise, the lines from *Satyre II*, which Harris cites, make the sardonic observation that the "starving" playwright, unseen by the audience, by his labor provides "ideot actors" with their livelihood. The opening lines of the poem—"Sir; though (I thanke God for it) I do hate / Perfectly all this towne"[11]—should discourage any simple identification of the speaker's views with those of the poet himself.

* * *

The *Holy Sonnet*, "This is my Playes last scene . . ." concludes:

> Impute me righteous, thus purg'd of evill,
> For thus I leave the world, the flesh, and devill.[12]

Gardner observes that these words recall "the renunciations which precede the administration of baptism in the Book of Common Prayer" (p. 67). On this hint, it is worth examining the sonnet as an imagined form of baptismal rite conducted, paradoxically, as an *exit*

---

[11] John T. Shawcross, ed., *The Complete Poetry of John Donne* (New York: Anchor Books, 1967), p. 18. Subsequent quotations are from this edition.

[12] Shawcross, p. 340. This sonnet is no. VI in Grierson's edition. Shawcross's reading of this couplet agrees with that of Gardner.

from the world—or from the stage of the speaker's "last scene"—
rather than, as is more usual of baptism, as an entrance to "this
great stage of fools," where, as Lear puts it, "we waul and
cry"(IV.vi.181; 178). The distressed speaker of the sonnet, who acknowledges his life's race has been "Idly, but quickly runne," faces
imminent death, pictured as a glutton ready to "unjoynt" his body
and soul as one might greedily tear apart a chicken or a capon, and
"feare," of "that face" after death, which already shakes every
joint—so much so, the conceit implies, that perhaps he will fall
apart, die, before glutton death can get him. This is a typically intense, witty, seemingly inescapable dilemma for a Donne persona in
the *Holy Sonnets*, generating profound "salvation anxiety."[13]

But there is yet more tension in the sonnet that arises from
standing expectation of the customary order of events on its head.
The only hope of the speaker is to be "purg'd of evill." For this to
happen the speaker must go through an emergency ritual renunciation of "the world, the flesh, and the devill." In the words of Cranmer's Catechism, "Baptism delivereth from death and the power of
the devil, and gyveth salvation and everlastynge lyfe to all them that
believe."[14] Donne uses this combination of world, flesh, devil, in
that order, only twice in his poetry. The other instance is in the
Holy Sonnet "Since she whome I lovd, hath payd her last debt"
which concludes "Least the World, fleshe, yea Devill putt thee
out."[15] In *Satyre III*, however, in an extended passage, in which the
"desperate coward" is addressed, knowledge of, and renunciation of
the "foes," that is, the "Devill," the world—its "parts" and its
"selfe"—and the flesh is enjoined.[16]

---

[13] An apt summary of Donne's personae in their spiritual agon, from
Margaret Edson's stage play, *Wit*.

[14] G. W. Bromily, *Baptism and the Anglican Reformers* (London:
Lutterworth, 1953), p. 179. The main lines of argument among the reformers concerned the "positive" and "negative" views of the efficacy of
baptism. On the positive side, baptism is entry into regenerate life; the
negative, it is seen as delivery from the devil, the world and the flesh. If
the speaker's plea in the sonnet reflects Donne's view, it puts him in the
conservative and "negative" camp. See pp. 180-181.

[15] Shawcross, p. 349. This sonnet is no. XVII in Grierson.

[16] Shawcross, pp. 23-24:

It has been noted that Shakespeare makes use of the renunciations of the baptism service in *Henry VIII* when he has Wolsey say,
"Vaine pomp and glory of this world, I hate ye" (III.ii.365). [17] More
interesting, however, in light of Donne's play with "world, flesh and
devil," is Shakespeare's extended descant on the theme in *I Henry
IV*, Act II, scene iv (the play-acting scene) beginning at the point
where the Prince proposes a reversal of roles: "Dost thou speak like
a king? Do thou stand for me, and I'll play my father"(417-418). In
the following forty-five lines the Prince and Falstaff enact a fore-
shadowing of the eventual rejection of Falstaff. It is, of course, a
superlative comic burlesque on several counts, that no modern production would consider excising.[18] Its structure is based upon a bril-
liantly clever reversal of the renunciations: Falstaff is ritually
rejected as devil, flesh and world, the modulation of ritual heard in
Falstaff's repetition at the conclusion of the sequence: "banish not

---

> O desperate coward, wilt thou seem bold, and
> To thy foes and his (who made thee to stand
> Sentinell in this world's garrison) thus yeeld,
> And for forbidden warres, leave th'appointed field?
> Know thy foes, the foule Devill h'is, whom thou
> Strivest to please: for hate, not love, would allow
> Thee faine, his whole Realme to be quit; and as
> The worlds all parts wither away and passe,
> So the worlds selfe, thy other lov'd foe, is
> In her decrepit wayne, and thou loving this,
> Dost love a wither'd and worne strumpet; last,
> Flesh (it selfes death) and joyes which flesh can taste,
> Thou lovest; and thy faire goodly soule, which doth
> Give this flesh power to taste joy, thou dost loath;
> Seek true religion. (29-43)

[17] John Henry Blunt, ed., *The Annotated Book of Common Prayer*
(London: Longmans, Green, 1903), p. 413.

[18] It was not always so highly prized. See S. B. Hemingway, ed., *The
New Variorum Henry IV, Part One*, (Philadelphia: Lippincott, 1936), p.
159. Eighteenth-century sentiment was generally against this scene, occasional revivals never producing the satisfaction that admirers of Shakespeare expected. Hemingway concludes, "the omission of the 'mock-trial'
is unthinkable to the 20th century playgoer or reader."

him thy Harry's company, banish not him thy Harry's company—banish plump Jack, and banish all the world"(460-462).

The first note in the solemn sequence is sounded in Falstaff's objection that Hal will not play the King so well as he has done: "Depose me? If thou dost it half so gravely, so majestically, both in word and matter, hang me up by the heels for a rabbit-sucker or a poulter's hare"(419-421). The suggestion of ludicrous inversion and the mental image of gigantic Falstaff, crowned and with scepter, perhaps recalling the popular woodcuts of the Devil as monarch of the world astride the globe, set this climactic section of the scene. Presently, the Prince, as his father, begins his denunciation: "Thou art violently carried away from grace. There is a devil haunts thee in the likeness of an old fat man" (430-432).

It is the Flesh, however, that appropriately occupies the central section of the charade-like performance as a cornucopia of vivid figures of grossness and gluttony characterize Falstaff's girth: a "tun of man," a "trunk of humours," "bolting hutch of beastliness" and so on to the memorable figure of the "roasted Manningtree ox with the pudding in his belly." In addition to the many editorial explications of this geographically specific image which mention, among other matters, the association of the town with morality plays and altercations with badly-behaved stage players,[19] it is possible that evocations of the belly of a beast and of roasting seem fitting for the sins and punishment of the Flesh.

The sequence concludes, necessarily, with the renunciation of the World—"all the world"—Falstaff. As if taking a solemn religious vow, the Prince's reply to Falstaff's plea is "I do, I will." The finality is underscored by knocking at the door, offstage, as the agents of justice arrive. Falstaff's indignant "play out the play. I have much to say in the behalf of that Falstaff" (465-466) capped by the Prince's "the devil rides upon a fiddle-stick" (469), which is glossed in the New Arden edition as "The Devil's leading this dance,"[20] is the brief coda that reminds us of the start of the sequence with the renunciation of the devil.

---

[19] See A. R. Humphreys, ed., *The First Part of King Henry IV* (London: Methuen, 1960) and David Bevington, ed., *Henry IV, Part I* (Oxford: Oxford University Press, 1987).

[20] Humphreys, p. 83.

If the rite of baptism plays the role that I have here outlined in this part of Act II, scene iv, it is also possible that its language of dying and rising again, as in the 1549 *Book of Common Prayer*, "dye from synne, and ryse agayne unto righteousnesse, continually mortifying all our euyll and corrupte affections,"[21] etc. prompted the episode of Falstaff's mock death on the battlefield—Prince: "Could not all this flesh / Keep in a little life?" (V.iv.102)—his rising again, and his comic vow to "purge, and leave sack" (V.iv.170). However, the language of the Prayer Books of 1549 and 1552 was so pervasive in the era of Donne and Shakespeare that it might be objected that evident echoes have no special critical force. Yet in the works discussed in this essay, the echoes are not accidental: they appear to be used in deliberate rhetorical reversions of expectation. It also appears that the echoes arise not from the Baptism rite proper. In the 1549, 1552, and 1559 Prayer Books the order of renunciation is sin, the world and the devil, but in the "Letany and Suffrages," one of the Deprecations reads "from fornicacion, and all other deadlye synne, and from al the decytes of the worlde, the fleshe, and the deuill: Good lorde deliuer vs."[22] The more graphic terms "fornication" and "deceit" are better suited to the Falstaff regime than merely "sin."

It is likely that the Litany formula superceded those of the Baptism rite in the public mind, perhaps because of Cranmer's "wonderfully sonorous language"[23] and the prominence and popularity of the new litany—it was to be performed on Sundays, Wednesdays and Fridays, whereas public baptisms were much more infre-

---

[21] Quotations are from facsimiles of the 1549 and 1552 *BCP*.

[22] *BCP*, 1549. The wording remains the same, with slight variations of spelling in the 1552 and 1559 versions. The wording of the public baptism ceremony, however, is subject to considerable change in subsequent versions, as is the rubric. Instruction to the priest for making the sign of the cross on forehead and breast in the 1549 version, for instance, is omitted from subsequent versions. Baptism was an especially contested matter.

[23] Diarmid MacCulloch, *Thomas Cranmer: A Life* (Yale: Yale University Press, 1996), pp. 328, 511. The Litany, published in 1544, was the first service authorized in England (p. 328).

quent[24]—even though it was now confined to the inside of church, as the reformers increasingly constrained the sacramental ceremonies.[25]

Donne could have seen *1 Henry IV* on stage in 1597, the likely date of the play's composition, before or after the Islands expedition, but there is no evidence that he did. Given the transformative power of his imagination, however, it is possible that he, a "great frequenter" in Baker's phrase, no "idle spectator," would have recognized Shakespeare's brilliant use of the renunciation pattern in *I Henry IV*. A similarly inventive use of the renunciation formula resolves the intense personal drama of the "last scene" of the play of his life in the Holy Sonnet. If this is so, and if the sonnet was in some way occasioned by a specific experience of the theater, it still retains the mystery of Donne's attitude to the theater. If he witnessed the renunciation of fat Jack, "all the world," Falstaff, did he "freely yield" to the experience, as Cruttwell suggests, or receive it with a "classical shudder"? Or both?

McMaster University

---

[24] John E. Booty, ed., *The Book of Common Prayer 1559: The Elizabethan Prayer Book* (Washington D.C.: Folger Shakespeare Library, 1976), p. 393.

[25] MacCulloch, p. 375.

Poetry, Patronage, and Identity in the Dance of the Graces, Book VI of *The Faerie Queene*

ALZADA TIPTON

THIS essay comes from a larger project on identity, poetry, and patronage in Book VI of *The Faerie Queene*, which returns to a question asked in the early twentieth century as to whom Sir Calidore might represent: Sidney or Essex. My answer is that he represents both, or, more specifically, that he represents an ideal that Sidney embodied, an ideal Spenser suggests to Essex as a corrective to his public identity. Spenser uses the common understanding of Sidney as combining both arms and arts in his life in order to hint to Essex that he needs to learn this balancing act, as Essex has emphasized the martial at the expense of the poetic. My analysis of the first eight cantos of the Book shows that they argue that martial ability is limited in scope and most important in the protection and patronage of poetry. My argument about the last four cantos is that they transform the patronage of poetry from a martial act to a poetic act; thus, Spenser shows Essex that patronizing a poet such as himself will give Essex access to the poetic process (without having to write poetry himself). Adding poetry to his list of accomplishments through his act of patronage, Essex will also open himself to learning all the general lessons about how to be a successful courtier that poetry such as *The Faerie Queene* can teach.

The most important representation of Essex's opportunity to draw upon Sidney's legacy occurs in Calidore's education in poetry on Mount Acidale. Calidore's witnessing of the dance of the Graces, their subsequent disappearance, Colin Clout's breaking his pipes in displeasure, and his conversation with Calidore have received a great deal of critical attention. The first thing that needs to be noted about this scene, however, is how much it empowers the poet. The poet is here shown to be the privileged participant in the creation of beauty and meaning, and, for the moment, the knight-patron is nothing more than a boorish interloper. Indeed, given Calidore's eagerness to take in the scene and his sorrow at his destruction of it, Colin's rather intimidating "fell despight / Of that displeasure"(VI.x.18.4-5)[1] seems less like an admission of the fragility of poetry and more like a threat that this precious commodity can be withheld at the will of the poet.[2] Derek Alwes has argued that Colin's description of the Graces' disappearance ("being gone, none can them bring in place, / But whom they of them selues list so to grace") testifies to the privileged status of the poet as the *only* one who can call them back, the only one who enjoys the favor of the graces. Furthermore, Calidore's mistaken understanding of Colin's words as saying that *nobody* can bring them back shows even more that Calidore is a "courtier in need of a poet's instruction."[3] Calidore's helplessness to understand what he has seen is emphasized; he "wist not what to weene" (VI.x.17.9) until Colin, "seeing him to mourne, / Drew neare, that he the truth of all by him mote learne" (VI.x.18.8-9). Colin "dilates" (VI.x.21.1) for eight stanzas on the meaning of the dance of the Graces and in doing so almost wins Calidore as a permanent pupil:

> In such discourses they together spent
> Long time, as fit occasion forth them led;
> With which the Knight him selfe did much content,
> And with delight his greedy fancy fed.

---

[1] All citations from Book VI of *The Faerie Queene* come from Edmund Spenser, *The Faerie Queene*, ed. A.C. Hamilton (London: Longman, 1977).

[2] In a related but differently oriented argument, Kelsey and Peterson have discussed how Spenser's several representations of Colin Clout breaking his pipe continue a long tradition from Roman poets of using this image to represent the poet's response to inadequate patronage. See Lin Kelsey and Richard Peterson, "Rereading Colin's Broken Pipe: Spenser and the Problem of Patronage," *Spenser Studies* 14 (2000): 233-72.

[3] Derek Alwes, "'Who knowes not Colin Clout?': Spenser's Self-Advertisement in *The Faerie Queene*, Book 6," *Modern Philology* 88, no. 1 (1990): 35.

Both of his words, which he with reason red;
And also of the place, whose pleasures rare
With such regard his sences rauished,
That thence, he had no will away to fare,
But wisht, that with that shepheard he mote dwelling
share. (IV.x.30.1-9)

The dance of the Graces itself further confirms the interpretation that Calidore learns about poetry on Mount Acidale. From C.
S. Lewis onward, critics have argued that the dance of the Graces
represents poetry. As Robert Stillman points out, "from the formal-
ist critics of the 1970s to the post-structuralist critics of the 1990s,
Spenserians have found on Mount Acidale an exemplary display of
la poesie pure."[4] Humphrey Tonkin discusses the similarity of
Mount Acidale to Parnassus.[5] He compares the ordering of the
dance by Colin's piping to Spenser's ordering of Faerie land by his
writing of the poem; the dance is the poem, and Calidore is the
reader, struggling to understand the vision of beauty that he sees.[6]
Richard Neuse discusses how poetry and courtesy are indistinguish-
able and says that courtesy "appears as the supreme *poetic* possibility in human existence, and as such represents the perfect point of
transition from (poet's) art to (reader's) life."[7] Daniel Javitch asserts
that the episode of the Graces "allegorizes Spenser's poetics."[8] Discussing the dance of the Graces, Michael O'Connell notes that the
echoes of Spenser's other poetry makes this scene "a glimpse of poetic inspiration and ideals," and more specifically a reference to
Spenser's "poetic career."[9] Elizabeth Bellamy finds the dance of the

---

[4] Robert Stillman, "Spenserian Autonomy and the Trial of New
Historicism: Book VI of *The Faerie Queene*," *English Literary
Renaissance* 22, no. 3 (1992): 299-314, 299-300.

[5] Humphrey Tonkin, *Spenser's Courteous Pastoral: Book Six of The
Faerie Queene* (Oxford: Clarendon Press, 1972), 126.

[6] Tonkin, 138-41.

[7] Richard Neuse, "Book VI as Conclusion to *The Faerie Queene*,"
ELH 35, no. 3 (1968): 329-53, 331.

[8] Daniel Javitch, *Poetry and Courtliness in Renaissance England*
(Princeton: Princeton Univ. Press, 1978), 147.

[9] Michael O'Connell, *Mirror and Veil: The Historical Dimension of
Spenser's Faerie Queene* (Chapel Hill: Univ. of North Carolina Press,
1977), 182.

Graces to be "a myth about the origins of poetry."[10] Even a less ide-
alizing reader of the Book finds a close connection between literary
issues and the events of the Book; Jacqueline Miller finds in Calidore Spenser's critical examination of how he has used the technique of allegory throughout the poem.[11]

At the same time, the dance of the Graces can be seen as specifically addressing the act of patronage. The arrangement of
Graces is always interpreted as indicating the acts of giving and receiving. E. K.'s gloss from the April eclogue of *The Shepheardes
Calendar* describes the Graces as:

> whom the poetes feyned to be the Goddesses of al
> bountie and comelines, which therefore (as sayth
> Theodontius) they make three, to wete, that men first
> ought to be gracious and bountiful to other freely, then
> to receive benefits as other mens hands courteously, and
> thirdly to requite them thankfully: which are three sun-
> dry Actions in liberalitye.[12]

The traditional arrangement, as it is in the April eclogue, has two
Graces facing toward the viewer and one facing away, suggesting,
again in E. K.'s words, that "double thanke to be due to us for the
benefit we have done."[13] This arrangement suggests the ample re-
wards the viewer (traditionally read as the original giver, the patron) receives for his support of poetry. The description of the
Graces in Book VI has traditionally been taken by critics to mean

---

[10] Elizabeth Bellamy, "Colin and Orphic Interpretation: Reading Neo-
platonically on Spenser's Acidale," *Comparative Literature Studies* 27, no.
3 (1990): 172-92, 172.

[11] Jacqueline Miller, "The Courtly Figure: Spenser's Anatomy of Allegory," *Studies in English Literature, 1500-1900* 31 (1991): 51-68.

[12] Edmund Spenser, *The Shepheardes Calendar*, from *The Works of
Edmund Spenser: A Variorum Edition*, eds. Edwin Greenlaw, Charles
Osgood, Frederick Padelford, and Ray Heffner (Baltimore: Johns Hop-
kins Univ. Press, 1938-47), vol. 7, parts 1 and 2 (*The Minor Poems*: vol. 1
and vol. 2), 44. Quotations from *Amoretti* 74 also come from these volumes.

[13] Ibid.

that the position of the Graces is reversed; there are now two Graces with their back to us and one facing the viewer:[14]

> That two of them still forward [read as froward] seem'd to bee,
> But one still towards shew'd her self afore;
> That good should from vs goe, then come in greater store.
> (VI.x.24.7-9)

If "forward" is changed to "froward," critics have suggested that the arrangement could mean that the viewer originates a double act of giving, which receives only half as much in return; the last line thus indicates that "good should from us go" *rather than* "come in greater store."[15] In the context of this argument, this rearrangement of the traditional configuration of the Graces could be seen as emphasizing the obligations of patronage; the patron needs to offer a greater quantity of the "good" of material support in order to receive the "good" of poetry. There is also the possibility, however, that the movement originates with the one Grace facing the viewer. This suggests an initial gift to the viewer/patron, which the viewer/patron then doubly repays. This interpretation suggests that the patron should recognize the gift of "Grace" that the poet has initially given to him or her and should doubly reward the poet. In either interpretation, however, it should be noted that the exchange with the poet *allows* a patron to "be" a Grace; if the Graces represent poetry and patronage, it is the patron's generous act of giving, presumably, material support that transforms that material support into poetic, transcendental, or divine form. Bates also suggests the possibility that "forward" should not be changed to "froward" and that all the Graces are facing outward, with their backs to one another. She says that this reading suggests that "the viewer is to expect not only 'double thanke' but a threefold reward for his pains, for each one of the Graces, when she comes round, looks out prom-

---

[14] See Catherine Bates, *The Rhetoric of Courtship in Elizabethan Language and Literature* (Cambridge: Cambridge Univ. Press, 1992), 154, note 36 for a listing of editors and critics that change "forward" to "froward." In her discussion, Bates suggests that the viewer could also be read as the poet (155); this claim is obviously inconsistent with my argument that the viewer is Sir Calidore (who is Essex).

[15] Bates, 154.

isingly to him."[16] This interpretation, too, fits well with the argument at hand, as it emphasizes the enormous value of the poetry given to the patron for his or her benefit. And finally, the fact, as Bates has noted, that all of these interpretations (as well as many more) can exist simultaneously in these three lines show the value of poetry—how much meaning it can pack into an economical package—and how that meaning can be transformative for a courtier/patron.

The exchanges between giver and recipient implied by the positions of the Graces have sometimes been connected to Spenser's image of giving and receiving from the Proem of Book VI, when he describes his relationship to the Queen. Spenser addresses the Queen on the issue of writing to her about a courtesy she already embodies:

> Then pardon me, most dreaded Soueraine,
> That from your selfe I doe this vertue bring,
> And to your selfe doe it returne againe:
> So from the Ocean all riuers spring,
> And tribute backe repay as to their King.
> Right so from you all goodly vertues well
> Into the rest, which round about you ring,
> Faire Lords and Ladies, which about you dwell,
> And doe adorne your Court, where courtesies excell.
> (Proem, 7.1-9)

The similarity between the ring of lords and ladies around the queen and the dance of the Graces is often noted,[17] and critics such as Bates see this moment as establishing Book VI's "main theme of thanks, reward, patronage, and gratitude"; Spenser is co-opting Elizabeth into a patronage relationship by establishing a complicated exchange between giver and recipient.[18] This argument is then used to discuss patronage relationships in Book VI as being between Spenser and Elizabeth.[19] However, it can be argued equally

---

[16] Bates, 155.

[17] Hamilton, 625.

[18] Bates, 157. See also Bates, 14.

[19] See Bates and Alwes. See also Margaret Hannay, "'My Sheep are Thoughts': Self-Reflexive Pastoral in *The Faerie Queene*, Book VI and the New Arcadia," *Spenser Studies* 9 (1988): 137-59.

plausibly that this passage is notably different from the dance of the Graces and the exchange between Calidore and Colin Clout. The *ideal* of exchange offered in the Proem (whether lived up to by Elizabeth in real life or not) is of an exchange that is not really an exchange; the lines between giver and recipient are blurred, the gifts offered are already owned, the exchange has not really altered the status quo. This is very different from Calidore in canto ten, who really seems to be lacking in knowledge or understanding of the Graces, who needs Colin's tutelage to understand what he has seen, and whose internal version of the virtue the Graces represent is drastically changed once he experiences the vision of the Graces and the exchange with Colin. The differences between the exchanges in the Proem and in canto ten demonstrate that Spenser is interested in persuading somebody other than Elizabeth as his patron in this Book. In the Proem's version of her as patron, she is not accessible by the poet because she does not need to be taught anything about courtesy or poetry—she is a *"peereles* Poetress"(l.576; my emphasis). Thus, this is the only book of *The Faerie Queene* that does not have a figure who represents Elizabeth in it; she is in the middle of the circle of lords and ladies at court in the Proem, but she is conspicuously *not* the woman in the middle of the ring that surrounds Pastorella or Colin's country lass. Her absence could be read as a criticism of her failure as a patron, but it also could be read as an indication that she is not the proper object of Spenser's quest for patronage because his arguments about the intellectual value of poetry cannot be applied to her. Also, she is not a proper patron for Spenser to pursue because she is Essex's patron;[20] the Graces teach "vs, how to each degree and kynde / We should our selues demeane, to low, to hie"(VI.x.23.7-8), and this knowledge points Spenser to Essex as the right "degree and kynde" to patronize him. Thus, the Proem sets up an absolute dividing line between Elizabeth and her court; the Proem describes courtesy in general as flourishing in Antiquity, whereas "in the present age" it has become "forgerie, / Fashion'd to please the eies of them, that pas / Which see not perfect things but in a glas"(5.3-5). Elizabeth,

---

[20]See Eleanor Rosenberg, *Leicester: Patron of Letters* (New York: Columbia Univ. Press, 1955) as the initial critic who discussed how the patronage of literature proceeded from the noblemen around Elizabeth, rather than Elizabeth herself.

however, offers a pattern of courtesy that cannot be found in Antiquity (stanza 6). Spenser thus announces that a Book offering instruction in courtesy (or patronage or poetry or virtue) is not aiming for Elizabeth as its reader. Instead, a more likely reader would be that nobleman who seems at one moment to be implicated in the corruption of the court that values "forgeries," and in another moment included in those "faire Lordes and Ladies, which about you dwell, / And doe adorne your Court, where courtesies excell"(7.8-9). The bifurcated presentation of the courtier implies that he is in need of Spenser's services and that, were he to take up those services, he could achieve an ideal that would allow him to "become" a Grace, inasmuch as he would the occupy the position of the three Graces surrounding their central figure and inspiration.

Thus, the Graces represent both poetry and patronage and, furthermore, show that patronage is poetry, that patronage invites the courtier to interact with the poet and to learn the ideas about values and identity that the poet embodies in poetry. These are ideas that the courtier/patron needs because they show him how to achieve the courtly identity best by learning about virtues such as holiness or temperance or chastity. But poetry also offers a huge range of insights about the political, social, economic, and ideological situations in which the courtier finds himself—in court, in government, in the city, in the nation, in Europe—and allows the courtier to navigate these contexts most successfully.[21] In this way, poetry is a valuable attribute itself—it shows that the courtier is well versed in arts as well as arms—but it also becomes a conduit for all kinds of instruction on the achieving of all kinds of virtue and of all kinds of successes. The wide range of meanings that critics have found in

---

[21] My argument here contends that all of the meanings that all critics of all schools have found in *The Faerie Queene* can fit under the rubric of things that it would be useful, profitable, and/or virtuous for a courtier to know. I feel that there is little use in making a distinction between moral value and Machiavellian utility as the intention of this text, as Spenser's poem allows for instruction in both kinds of arenas for the courtier. Similarly, the question as to what Spenser intends for his poetry at this moment in his career is not answered by an either/or choice between inward contemplation of virtue or outward activity in the life of court. Both are things that the courtier needs access to; both are provided to him by poetry.

the Graces is itself an example of the instructive possibilities of poetry: interpretations of the Graces range from theology to philosophy to politics to aesthetics. Robert Stillman describes the dance, "from sources both classical and Christian, esoteric lore out of Plato, Plotinus, and Ficino structures a mythic vision at once cosmic in its scope, political in its intention, and intensely private in its focus."[22] As M. M. Beard sums them up, the Graces can represent courtesy, the civilizing influence of beauty, the Christian notion of grace, and the Classical image of perfection, all at the same time.[23] Lila Geller has argued for an interpretation of the "fourth Grace," the woman in the middle of the circle, that understands her as an "encyclopaedic symbol for the sum of all arts and learning."[24] However, this seems a useful way of understanding the entire dance of the Graces, or even poetry itself, as one considers the enormous variety of ideas and issues Spenser includes in his education of the gentlemanly reader he intends to fashion through the course of *The Faerie Queene*. In this way, the dance of the Graces demonstrates to the courtier/patron/reader what the poet has to offer him in the intellectual exchange of patronage. In fact, the very multiplicity of possible interpretations of the Graces proves both the worthiness of the courtly reader to be enriched by this scene (he knows the value of the surplus of meaning in the scene) and the dependence of the courtly reader on an expert guide through it (he knows that he does not know as much as the poet about that meaning). Critics such as Bellamy and Hannay have discussed how Book VI not only teaches its reader about ideas such as Neoplatonism or the pastoral, but also teaches its reader how to *read* correctly—the Book instructs the reader in interpretation while it instructs the reader in Soul and Mind, or the relations between monarch and subject.

The transformation of patronage from chivalry to poetry, from protection to instruction, in the movement from the first eight cantos to the last four is most clearly signaled by the presence of the Graces and how they alter Calidore and his subsequent actions, but this transformation is also echoed in a number of smaller ways. A

---

[22] Stillman, 310.

[23] M. M. Beard, "Pastoralism as a Statemen of Value: *The Faerie Queene*, Book VI," *English Studies in Africa* 27, no. 2 (1984): 77-92, 90.

[24] Lila Geller, "The Acidalian Vision: Spenser's Graces in Book VI of *The Faerie Queene*," *Review of English Studies* 23 (1972): 267-77, 272.

detail that enacts the transformation of patronage from chivalry to poetry is the simile that likens the dance of the Graces to Ariadne's crown:

> Looke how the Crowne, which Ariadne wore
> Vpon her yuory forehead that same day,
> That Theseus her vnto his bridale bore,
> When the bold Centaures made that bloudy fray,
> With the fierce Lapithes, which did them dismay;
> Being now placed in the firmament,
> Through the bright heauen doth her beams display,
> And is vnto the starres an ornament,
> Which round about her moue in order excellent. (VI.x.13.1-9)

Numerous critics have noted the move towards transcendence in the stanza, which removes the crown from the arena of mortal struggle and places it in the immutable "firmament," but the changes that Spenser makes to the story of Ariadne and Theseus more clearly make it an allegory of patronage. Specifically, Ariadne is given the crown by Theseus, rather than Bacchus. With her crown associating her with poetry's tendency towards "stellification,"[25] Ariadne can be seen as a figure for poetry, as are all other women in this Book. Furthermore, she had previously aided Theseus by giving him a ball of string to unwind as he entered into the labyrinth to fight the Minotaur; in this way, she can be seen as representing the interpretive power of poetry to unravel mysteries, as Colin does for Calidore. Also, the fact that, later in her story, she is abandoned by Theseus might make her akin specifically to Serena. Theseus represents the courtier/patron much better than Bacchus, as he is both an adventuring knight and a great lord, rather than a god representing principles of revelry and ecstasy. That the crown is connected to Ariadne's and Theseus's "bridale" emphasizes the uniting of the couple, rather than their eventual separation; the image of transcendence comes from the union of poetry and patron, or at least from the moment of the patron's fidelity to poetry. Also, this version of the story has the fight between the Centaurs and the Lapithes happen during Theseus's "bridale" but keeps him out of it;

---

[25] Patrick Cheney, "The Old Poet Presents Himself: *Prothalamion* as a Defense of Spenser's Career," *Spenser Studies* 8 (1987): 211-38, 227.

instead of fighting on the behalf of the Lapithes in loyalty to his friends, this version removes the elements of violence and masculine bonds and shows Theseus only as the wooer and winner of poetry, commemorating their union by crowning her for eternity.

Another much-noted aspect of the dance of the Graces also signals the move from material power to intellectual inspiration in the priorities for poetry, and that is the shift in the identity of the fourth Grace in Spenser's poetry. In the April eclogue of *The Shepheardes Calendar*, Elizabeth was the fourth Grace, seated in the center of the circle and surrounded by the other Graces. In Book VI, the Fourth Grace is a country lass, not the Queen. On one level, this can be seen as reflecting Essex's rather precarious status as a client himself in a somewhat vexed patron/client relationship with the Queen. Her absence from this Book might be seen as implying Spenser's sympathy for Essex that his patron is, literally, not there for him when he needs her. However, this change from the Queen to a country lass also transforms the person in the center from the woman with the most power and wealth to the woman who represents poetic inspiration. Elizabeth is first presented in the Proem in the center of the ring, as we have seen. Once Calidore enters the pastoral world, however, she disappears, and, in fact, Spenser underlines her absence, however apologetically (VI.x.28). In canto ix, Calidore sees first Pastorella in the center of a ring of shepherds and shepherdesses and then the country lass is placed in the center of the Graces;[26] both of these are figures whose beauty, virtue, and grace represent pastoral poetry and poetic inspiration.[27] In *Amoretti* #74, Spenser suggests a similar move away from poetry as the object of material support to poetry as intellectual activity. He calls the three Elizabeths in his life "three such graces" who have given him "giufts of body, fortune, and of mind" (1.4). His mother initially gave him the gift of life, and Elizabeth Tudor has given him "giufts of fortune"—she is the patron "that honour and large richesse to me lent"(1.8). This makes Elizabeth Boyle the one who gave him the gifts of the mind, who encouraged his poetry by inspiring it: "by whom my spirit out of dust was raysed: / to speake her prayse and glory excellent, / of all alive most

---

[26] Beard, 86.
[27] Geller, 53.

worthy to be praysed" (ll.9-11). Thus, there is a movement in this poem from liberality in providing honor and riches to liberality in providing poetic inspiration that is very similar to the shifting figure of the woman in the middle of the various rings of Book VI of *The Faerie Queene.*

Perhaps the most important proof that Spenser advocates for the transformative power of poetry for the patron comes in the record of Calidore's achievements after his education in poetry on Mount Acidale. David Miller demonstrates how Calidore and Colin together make up the entirety of Orpheus: "one pipes to the dance; the other descends to the underworld, rescues Pastorella, tames the hellish hound."[28] Miller argues that the splitting of Orpheus into two people demonstrates the disjunction between the contemplative and the active lives, but one could argue that the relationship is less of disjunction than cause and effect. As Robert Stillman puts it,

> only because Calidore has seen Colin's poetic vision, Spenser's allegorical logic suggests, is he able to complete his quest, the rescue of Pastorella from the brigants and the imprisonment (however temporary) of the Blatant Beast. The reciprocity essential to Spenser's understanding of courtesy, a virtue that entails both giving and receiving, binds poet to hero.[29]

Notably, immediately after his time on Mount Acidale, Calidore saves Pastorella from a tiger (VI.x.34-6). This incident combines the chivalric and pastoral worlds in a new way, suggesting that the patron who receives instruction from the poet will be successful in all arenas. Calidore shows martial courage when confronting the tiger and at the same time uses a "shepheards hooke"(VI.x.35.1), his only weapon, to dispatch it. He saves Pastorella, the embodiment of the pastoral, and, in doing so, gives her a new appreciation of the martial endeavors she had previously ignored: "from that day forth she gan him to affect, / And daily more her fauour to augment" (VI.x.37.1-2). Even the cowardly actions of Coridon testify

---

[28] David L. Miller, "Abandoning the Quest," *ELH* 46 (1979): 173-92, 189.

[29] Stillman, 312-3.

to the superiority of the combination of arms and arts in the court-ier/patron; as a suitor to Pastorella (poetry) who is only a shepherd, Coridon is shown to be weak, jealous, and ineffective. Calidore is a knight again, and a much more successful one than any time since the beginning of the Book, but he is so because he performs his knightly deeds in the service of the pastoral and because he incor-porates elements of the pastoral in those deeds.

This point is underlined again when Calidore rescues Pastorella from the Brigants.[30] He wears his armor under his shepherds' clothes (VI.xi.36), and he ingratiates himself with the Brigants and learns strategic information from them by offering to take care of their sheep for them (VI.xi.39-41). He then rescues Pastorella through his martial abilities, first by using the "sword of meanest sort"(VI.xi.42.6) that he has acquired and then by using a "sword of better say" (VI.xi.47.5) that he finds among the carcasses of the Brigants he has slain. The fact that he gets a better sword suggests that Calidore's chivalric identity has been changed and improved; the fact that he acquires this sword during his rescue of Pastorella, and "inherits" it from the dead, might possibly suggest Sidney's provision in his will that left Essex his best sword. At the same time, the way the poem tells the story of Calidore and Pastorella suggests the story of Persephone and Hades, Orpheus and Eury-dice, or even Christ's harrowing of Hell; this martial or chivalric moment has multiple poetic meanings to it. After his rescue of her, Calidore appears as the accepted suitor of Pastorella, and this reso-lution of the relationship suggests the ideal union of the chivalric and the pastoral that the Book has advocated in its last four cantos. At the moment of this union, we are also reminded of Calidore's status as a patron. He returns to the Brigants' cave to remove their "spoyles and threasures"(VI.xi.51.2) in order to bestow them on Pastorella, and he gives the flocks of sheep taken from Melibee to

---

[30] The Brigants could be seen as Spenser's version of a different kind of patron, whose interest lies solely in the economics of the exchange. This interpretation is suggested by Spenser's emphasis on the financial transac-tions of the Brigants with the merchants who come to purchase the shep-herds and shepherdesses as slaves and who are able to pinpoint their value precisely (VI.xi.10-4).

Coridon.[31] Furthermore, Calidore's status as *aristocratic* patron is underlined when he transports Pastorella to the Castle of Belgard, thus allowing her to discover her noble parentage; he has placed the pastoral where it is "cherish[ed] with all things choice and rare" (VI.xii.14.7) by the brave knight and beautiful lady who gave it life. And, finally, the rescue of Pastorella also seems to remind Calidore of his duty to the Faerie Queene, and his quest for the Blatant Beast is very quickly ended successfully. Calidore defeats the Blatant Beast with only his shield (VI.xii.30). This detail emphasizes the protective rather than the aggressive aspect of Calidore's armor; in doing so, it perhaps recalls the first eight cantos' insistence on the necessity for the knight/patron to protect poetry, especially from the vituperation that the Blatant Beast represents.

Having made his case to Essex for the mutual benefits that would arise from a patronage relationship, Spenser refuses to end the Book on a note of triumph or finality: Calidore and Pastorella (like Redcrosse and Una) do not actually get married, and the Blatant Beast gets loose and roams the world again. Perhaps this suggests that Spenser ends the Book in such an incomplete way in order to indicate to Essex that the next move is his; once Spenser has made the argument for Essex's patronage, it is up to Essex to initiate the relationship. Certainly, the Book implies, if he were to do so he would be insuring his success as a courtier while cherishing the precious art of poetry.

Hamline University

---

[31] It is interesting that the transformation of patronage into an intellectual act cannot completely ignore the economics of the relationship. Perhaps this moment is Spenser's acknowledgement that everybody has to get their living somehow. There certainly seems to be a difference between Calidore's gifts to Pastorella and Coridon, and the Brigants' assessment of Pastorella's worth on the market, or even Calidore's previous attempt to put a monetary value on the pastoral space when he tries to pay Melibee. Here, the gift of treasure to Pastorella seems part of Calidore's wooing of her, and the gift of the sheep to Coridon allows him to continue as the sole remaining legacy of Melibee's world.

The "Allurement of Liking" and the "Contentation of the Eyes": Decoding the Visual Culture of the Elizabethan Prodigy House

JAMES M. SUTTON

RECENT investigations into the visual culture of early modern England have begun to recover the fascinating yet now remote ways that men and women of that period quite literally *viewed* their world. Although work in this vein has already reinvigorated the kinds of questions we ask of portraits, maps, prints, collections of curiosities and even everyday material objects, and the relationships of race, gender and colonization to these items seen and touched, the field of visual culture still affords many open vistas.[1] For example, we still have much to learn about how early modern men and women *saw* architecture. I wish to make some preliminary proposals about the visual experience of one kind of Elizabethan building, the class of especially large country homes—often called "prodigy houses" in the literature—constructed in the 1560s, 1570s and 1580s by a few magnates and councilors in order to promote themselves and attract the queen while on summer progress.[2] I should add that, because my observations are derived from

---

[1] See for example, the essays collected in Peter Erickson and Clark Hulse, eds., *Early Modern Visual Culture: Representation, Race and Empire in Renaissance England* (Philadelphia: Univ. of Pennsylvania Press, 2000); and Patricia Fumerton and Simon Hunt, eds., *Renaissance Culture and the Everyday* (Philadelphia: Univ. of Pennsylvania Press, 1999).

[2] The term "prodigy house" seems to originate from the noted architectural historian, Sir John Summerson. It defines the very largest country houses of the era, those edifices like Christopher Hatton's Holdenby,

what is ostensibly a congratulatory letter from one Elizabethan magnate to another on his fine new house, what I recover in this essay are the visual attitudes and experiences of an elite coterie of courtier-councilors who enjoyed enormous privileges (economic, political and cultural) that enabled (if not compelled) them to build "to envious show." Here I primarily venture the insider's view of the ostentatious, palatial Elizabethan country home; although I conclude with the views of two outsiders—a map-maker and a gardener—who commented on a particularly significant prodigy home, a full investigation of external, extramural reaction to these show houses lies beyond the scope of this exploratory essay.[3]

At some point during August 1579, William Cecil, Lord Burghley paid an overnight visit to Holdenby, a Northamptonshire country house built by his friend and co-councilor, Christopher Hatton, in open and clear emulation of Burghley's own Hertfordshire residence, Theobalds.[4] Hatton seems not to have been present

---

William Cecil's Theobalds and Burghley House, Robert Dudley's Kenilworth, and Thomas Cecil's Wimbledon House which Summerson claimed "were built or enlarged specifically as places in which to receive the Queen, as tributes and monuments of loyalty." *Architecture In Britain 1530-1830* (Harmondsworth: Penguin Books, Ltd, 1953; rev. ed. 1983), 63.

[3] I hope to provide a more comprehensive examination of alternative and less celebratory kinds of vision, especially as they relate to William Cecil's Theobalds, in my forthcoming *The Poetics and Politics of Display at an Early Modern Prodigy House: The Cecils at Theobalds, 1564-1607* (Aldershot, Burlington, VT and Singapore: Ashgate Publishing Limited, 2003). This investigation will incorporate the views of those throngs kept outside the estate's gates (the local lower gentry; merchants, shop-keepers and apprentices from neighboring towns and villages; the laboring poor, vagrants, and maimed veterans), and the opinions of those men and women who were permitted entry only so that they could perform the myriad types of work that these proxy palaces required in order to function.

[4] For a description of Elizabethan Holdenby, see Mark Girouard, *Town and Country* (New Haven and London: Yale Univ. Press, 1992), 197-210. For a comparison of Hatton's house to Cecil's, see Malcolm Airs, "'Pomp or Glory': The Influence of Theobalds," in *Patronage, Culture and Power: The Early Cecils, 1558-1612*, ed. Pauline Croft (New Haven and London: Yale Univ. Press, 2002), 7-8.

during the visit, and Burghley, assuming the role of architectural critic, wrote to Hatton of his impressions of the estate. Although, on its surface, this letter is little more than a generic early modern thank-you note, its depths reveal much more. Within lie hints of the visual thinking and "building codes"—those shared habits of mind, patterns of design, and attitudes towards material that could shape undeveloped rural space into tautly defined architectural space—that Cecil, Hatton and a few others followed when fabricating their massive homes. Burghley recalled that,

> approaching to the house, being led by a large, long, straight fair way, I found a great magnificence in the front or front pieces of the house, and so every part answerable to other, to allure liking. I found no one thing of greater grace than your stately ascent from your hall to your great chamber; and your chamber answerable with largeness and lightsomeness, that truly a Momus could find no fault. I visited all your rooms, high and low, and only the contentation of mine eyes made me forget the infirmity of my legs.[5]

"To allure liking" and "the contentation of mine eyes": if we want to understand Elizabethan building practices and objectives, we must begin by unpacking these two suggestive phrases, which lie not just at the heart of Burghley's report of his seemingly self-guided tour of Hatton's Holdenby, but at the core of virtually every major architectural project, both urban and rural, of the period. The objective of country houses like Holdenby and Theobalds, as well as many town houses and civic monuments such as town halls and mercantile exchanges, was to attract attention unto themselves.[6] But

---

[5] H. Nicholas, *Memoirs of Sir Christopher Hatton* (London, 1847), 126.

[6] The bibliography for the period's country houses is vast. Among the standard texts are Summerson, *Architecture in Britain*, 39-98; Malcolm Airs, *The Making of the English Country House, 1500-1640* (London: Architectural Press, 1975); Mark Girouard, *Life in the English Country House: A Social and Architectural History* (New Haven and London: Yale Univ. Press, 1978), 81-118; Girouard, *Robert Smythson and the Elizabethan Country House* (New Haven and London: Yale Univ. Press, 1983); Timothy Mowl, *Elizabethan and Jacobean Style* (London: Phaidon

Burghley's choice of phrasing is much richer than this suggests; "allure" hints at more exotic, even dangerous realms, and "contentation" contains lost meanings that work against such exoticism. Allure suggests enchantment and magic, as if the house intended to cast a spell over its visitor. The agency, and the power, in this equation between house and viewer lies almost wholly with the house, the material object.[7] It demands or calls forth a gaze; it insists upon being scrutinized. Here, the gaze is not random. It is fixed and controlled. Furthermore, the viewer is caught up in a quasi-erotic system of desire: what is "allured" is "liking," which I take to be something far more than just mild-mannered appreciation. This "liking" certainly embraces appreciation and approval, but it shades into realms that suggest appropriation, jealousy, envy and desire. In short, Holdenby and all other comparable monu-

---

Books, 1993); and Colin Platt, *The Great Rebuildings of Tudor and Stuart England: Revolutions in Architectural Taste* (London: UCL Press, 1994), 1-132. On English town halls and civic architecture, see Robert Tittler, *Architecture and Power: The Town Hall and the English Urban Community, c. 1500-1640* (Oxford: Oxford Univ. Press, 1991); and Maurice Howard, "Classicism and Civic Architecture in Renaissance England," in *Albion's Classicism: The Visual Arts in Britain, 1550-1660*, ed. Lucy Gent (New Haven and London: Yale Univ. Press, 1995), 29-49. On the development of the major civic mercantile exchange in England, see several of the essays in Ann Saunders, ed., *The Royal Exchange* (London: The London Topographical Society, 1997), 3-118. For more recent theoretical work on the self-conscious display evident in much Elizabethan architecture, see Maurice Howard, "Self-Fashioning and the Classical Moment in Mid-Sixteenth-Century Architecture," in *Renaissance Bodies: The Human Figure in English Culture, c. 1540-1660*, ed. Lucy Gent and Nigel Llewellyn (London: Reaktion Books, 1990), 198-217; and Christy Anderson, "Learning to Read Architecture in the English Renaissance" in *Albion's Classicism*, 239-86.

[7] As will be seen, my own approach here is indebted to recent work on the material culture of Renaissance England. See especially Gloria Kury, "'Glancing Surfaces': Hilliard, Armour, and the Italian Model," in *Albion's Classicism*, 395-426; Margreta de Grazia, Maureen Quilligan, and Peter Stallybrass, ed., *Subject and Object in Renaissance Culture* (Cambridge: Cambridge Univ. Press, 1996); Lena Cowen Orlin, ed., *Material London, ca. 1600* (Philadelphia: Univ. of Pennsylvania Press, 2000); and Ann Rosalind Jones and Peter Stallybrass, *Renaissance Clothing and the Materials of Memory* (Cambridge: Cambridge Univ. Press, 2000).

ments of Elizabethan architecture aimed at producing the "allurement of liking." Each Elizabethan country house purposed the in-
citement of intense wonder, amazement and admiration in its
onlooker,[8] a sort of appreciation that could easily merge into a desire for possession and ownership if it were not for various systems
of control and restraint that tempered and frustrated such desire
within the viewer, reminding him that this was someone else's
house.

The remainder of Burghley's passage provides testimony to such
restraining codes, conventions of building and material display that
effectively worked to control the eye of the beholder and consequently temper his "liking." Among such conventions were a "large,
long, straight fair way," an "approach" to the house that underscores
the owner's agency. Hatton has inscribed the landscape with his
own authority by insisting that the entrance to his estate is simultaneously regularized and of considerable duration. In creating such a
drive, Hatton marks his possession via the implicit logic of the
threshold: Burghley is already experiencing the power of Holdenby
as he approaches the house. The fact that he elides any mention of
an actual, material threshold—no gates or lodges are recalled—does
not matter: once Cecil is "approaching" on that "fair way," he is in
Hatton's domain, a fact signaled clearly by his passive verbal construction, "being led." The choice of approach, and all the particular
factors that might go into manufacturing it, are here construed as
being Hatton's alone.

When Burghley arrives, finally, at the house, and faces its fa-
cade(s), he finds "a great magnificence in the front or front pieces
. . . and so every part answerable to other." The seeming vagueness
of this description masks a wealth of significant information.[9] Holdenby's face displays grandeur and opulence, but in a decorous

---

[8] Christy Anderson argues that "discovery, wonder and amazement
were all common categories used in the appreciation of architecture during
the sixteenth and seventeenth centuries." Anderson, 263 and passim.

[9] The vagueness of description here stems, I believe, not so much from
Burghley's inability to report accurately where he is and what he sees, but
rather from his implicit understanding and acceptance of the building
codes that mark the place as Hatton's. Too much description would verge
on, or smack of appropriation, so the lack of detail is in itself symptomatic
of Burghley's restraint.

manner. As with so much in this seemingly simple letter, "magnificence" becomes in my reading actually a carefully determined word, suggesting all that is proper and expected in the performance of English nobility in this period. Inasmuch as Hatton is magnificent, so too appears his house.[10] The precise location of such greatness, however, cannot be ascribed to just one part of the home's exterior: it appears in "the front or front pieces." What we discover here, using Burghley as our guide, is that monumental Elizabethan architecture worked on the principle of multiple rather than single facades. Holdenby had several major presentational compositions on its exterior, not just one. Like a hydra, the house had several material faces, and the one(s) the beholder viewed depended largely upon his status and the corresponding freedom of movement around the edifice.[11] Furthermore, each of these faces intended a performance of magnificence, a notion captured by Burghley's secondary phrasing, "front[is]pieces," a term with strong theatrical as well as architectural connotations in this period. Each "front" aimed to put on a show, whether as scenic backdrop for potential dramatic entertainments of the Queen or court on progress, or, as upon the occasion of Burghley's more staid, quiet visit, as architectural, material actors attesting to Holdenby's overall splendor.[12] Finally, these

---

[10] For a consideration of Renaissance magnificence as it relates to an earlier Florentine family also much concerned with self-promotion through architecture, see Dale Kent, *Cosimo de' Medici and the Florentine Renaissance: The Patron's Oeuvre* (New Haven and London: Yale Univ. Press, 2000), 214.

[11] My choice of metaphor is intentional and I hope suggestive. "Correct" viewing—that practiced and encoded by Burghley and Hatton and their elite friends—evaded the astonishing effects of the hydra's gaze. Burghley, who knows how to look at Holdenby, will not be turned to stone, frozen in wonder, by the edifice; rather he will keep moving, exploring the home with appreciative, collusive glances. Those outsiders who do not belong to the elite circle will suffer the fate of amazement, literally stopped in their tracks by the magnificence of what they see. Holdenby's splendor, then, can be appreciated and simultaneously transgressed by those in the know; others are to be repelled by this grandeur.

[12] Lucy Gent claims that "for England in the later sixteenth century the idea of a building as a clothed scaffold is suggestive. In surviving artefacts of that English culture textured surfaces are what impress: needlework tapestry, painted cloth, pargetting, brickwork, black and white timber fa-

several facades were "answerable [one] to [the] other," a phrase we must not equate with the tyranny of Italianate classical symmetry.[13] The several faces of Holdenby were comparable, but not identical, to each other; they bore a clear family resemblance, but they sported individual features, too. This fact cannot be overemphasized: "answerable" suggests a pleasing variety of likeness, not an absolute similarity. Such a virtuoso display, in which everything holds together despite differences, stands as a central tenet of the Elizabethan architectural code.[14] As Burghley's report indicates, it

---

cades, even windows. The front of Hardwick Hall for example, is made up of planes that are textured and shifting rather than structural. Surfaces are what seem to count." "'The Rash Gazer': Economies of Vision in Britain, 1550-1660," in *Albion's Classicism*, 381. I would add that Hardwick, like Holdenby and Burghley's Theobalds, presents not just one such shifting surface, but four, and that the distinctions between each "facade" there are notoriously difficult to draw due to the building's massing.

[13] While many Elizabethan buildings made use of classical elements, especially the loggia and the orders, employment of this vocabulary remained largely ornamental and decorative rather than thorough-going and integral. This is particularly the case with "symmetry," whether external or internal. While Palladio made an organizational principle of the concept in his villas, contemporary English practice eschewed the concept. Even in the famed country houses associated with Robert Smythson—Longleat, Wollaton, Hardwick—their symmetrical classicizing facades have almost no bearing on the internal plan. For further commentary on the relationship of English architecture to continental practices, see Alice Friedman, *House and Household in Elizabethan England: Wollaton Hall and the Willoughby Family* (Chicago: Univ. of Chicago Press, 1989), 71-134; David Evett, *Literature and the Visual Arts in Tudor England* (Athens, GA and London: Univ. of Georgia Press, 1990), 10-77; Howard, 201-7; and Anderson, 239-86.

[14] Maurice Howard helpfully comments that "[t]he significance of this architecture is made more complex because the variety of both written commentaries on classicism and the fantasising that took hold of its vocabulary of ornament in the decades after the 1550s met up with the revival of medievalism as a renewed mark of aristocratic respectability. Two examples can demonstrate this. Both Sir William Cecil and Sir Thomas Smith, key figures as secretaries to the governments of Edward VI's reign, began work on their major houses within . . . the period of restrained style of the mid-century. The final result, however, after twenty years of building . . . at Cecil's Burghley House [was a] building where the architectural

was precisely such a show of variety and conceit that created the "allurement of liking."

Having indicated in three short but powerful lines that the exterior of Hatton's house "allured liking," Cecil then reports on his tour of the home's interior. Again, despite the brevity of these remarks and their many silences, his comments are packed with significance, revealing much about how elite Elizabethans envisioned interior hierarchies of space. Burghley begins by congratulating Hatton upon the "grace" of "your stately ascent from your hall to your great chamber." The triple repetition of "your" should not be overlooked, nor should Cecil's interest in the "stately ascent." Read metaphorically as a conceit, country houses like Holdenby (and Burghley's own pair of mansions, Burghley House in Northamptonshire and Theobalds in Hertfordshire) were concerned primarily with "stately ascent," the gracious, decorous rising up of the nouveau riche; these homes were intended to figure such political and social climbing in aesthetic and cultural terms, however vested.[15] Read structurally and architecturally, Burghley's emphasis on the "stately ascent" points up both the greater importance of rooms located on floors above ground level, and the necessity that any home concerned with "rising up" have at least one staircase that literally, materially celebrated such physical movement upward through the home. Furthermore, the beginning and end points of Cecil's ascending trajectory—the "hall" and the "great chamber" respectively—reflect the well-documented shift in precedence and prestige of these spaces during the sixteenth century. For Cecil as for Hatton, the Great Chamber represented the true showcase of the home, where aesthetic, political, and familial display should all be carefully woven together. The hall had become something of an empty signifier, indicating if anything the householder's lip-service

order has been made complex, dependent on various sources and . . . deliberately archaising, referring to earlier complexities of ornament and therefore enlarging on their imaginative scope. Novelty here is not so much a search for a coherent use of classical order but a resume of the multi-layered discussion about classical ornament and its various possible meanings." Howard, 207.

[15] Both Hatton and Cecil were relatively new, "made men," politician-bureaucrats who did very well for themselves and their families due to their dedicated service to the ever-more-centralized Tudor state.

to older communal values. The real action occurred in the Great Chamber, a less public but far more ceremonial and even aulic space.[16] Burghley's remarks underscore this perfectly: he mentions the hall but says nothing of it, yet he comments on how the Chamber's "largeness and lightsomeness" make it "answerable." True, he utters not a word of description about the room's actual decoration (nothing about painting or paneling, wainscoting or mantles, ceiling decoration or interior sculptural effects), but his two qualifiers, general though they may be, speak volumes. Size and lighting effects matter—in fact, they matter so much to Elizabethans that they become, in and of themselves, material effects.[17] As the most significant room in the house, it is safe to assume that Holdenby's Great Chamber was among the largest and most heavily fenestrated spaces in the house. We have here, in short, the general recipe for a successful Elizabethan Great Chamber: elevation, maximum fenestration, and expansiveness (in length, width and height). The actual specifics of the room's appearance, and the general disposition of the movables and other objects, are of less overall importance than the fact that Hatton's Chamber meets the coded expectations of excellence and is, therefore, "answerable" to Cecil. The (textual) appearance of "Momus"—the Greek arch-critic and mythical scowler—at the very moment at which Burghley congratulates Hatton on his excellent Chamber, reflects yet again the room's superiority and preeminence, for Burghley calls upon Momus only to silence him: this most demanding and potentially damning of critics "could find no fault."

Having dismissed the critical mode in banishing Momus, Burghley concludes with more epideictic rhetoric. Humorously and in self-deprecating fashion, he writes that "I visited all your rooms,

---

[16] See Girouard, 1978, 84-94, for more general comments on this shift in taste.

[17] For a postmodern theorization of the role size might play in the appreciation of architecture, see Rem Koolhaas, *Small, Medium, Large, Extra-large* (New York: Monacelli Press, 1995). On the significance of illumination in the Elizabethan visual arts, see Kury, who in speaking of Hilliard's miniatures claims that "[c]hoice and handling of materials are uppermost in his thoughts, are in a sense his thoughts, and should be regarded as agents of culture. Light, rather than space, is the matrix of Hilliard's art, and arguably the principal source of its meaning." Kury, 416.

high and low, and only the contentation of mine eyes made me forget the infirmity of my legs." In denying Momus, Burghley also
seems to suddenly deny his own descriptive faculties; he claims to
have visited "all your rooms," but does not utter a word about how
they were arranged or how they appeared. Perhaps, as a close friend
and elite insider writing to the home's ultimate insider, Burghley
feels no need to describe the aspect of these hundreds of spaces. It
is enough to claim that he viewed them: too much description
might be construed as a gesture of appropriation. Thus Burghley's
"high and low" adequately fulfills his task, indicating that he thoroughly experienced the home and well comprehended the spatial
hierarchies it inscribes. Just as the terms "largeness" and "lightsomeness" participate in an elite Elizabethan shorthand embedding
lush materiality, the phrase "high and low" encodes an understanding of an exclusive Elizabethan poetics of space shared by Hatton,
Burghley, and other builders of sizeable prodigy houses. Burghley's
joke about the "infirmity of his legs" registers in another manner
the size of Holdenby: it takes some considerable physical effort to
view the whole house, as one must move both horizontally and ver-
tically through vast tracts of architecturalized space. Again, size
matters greatly in the building code for such houses, and Burghley's
tired legs are a sign that Hatton has clearly understood this. Moreover, the trade-off for physical exhaustion proves to be the further
stimulation of visual pleasure: the "contentation of mine eyes" casts
his fatigue into oblivion. On its surface, this phrase powerfully recalls and recasts "to allure liking," reinforcing that the pleasures—
the "contentations" or allurements—of a place like Holdenby are
primarily visual.

And yet, Burghley's strange phrasing here turns out to be at
least doubly suggestive, for "contentation" not only evokes the
pleasure, delight, joy, and wonder created in the viewer gazing at
Holdenby, it also subtly connotes the restraint necessary to such
viewing. While the word is now largely obsolete, in the Elizabethan
period it had a rich nexus of meanings. Most of these connotations
pointed to contentment, pleasure and satisfaction,[18] but at least two
were otherwise directed. The word could also mean "the contenting

---

[18] See the *Oxford English Dictionary*, (Oxford, 1971), 898, cons. 1a, 2,
3a, 3b, and 4.

oneself or one's mind with what one has; acquiescence in or acceptance of the situation;"[19] or "the satisfying of the conscience, of the
moral or rational faculty; the allaying of scruple or doubt."[20] Thus
the "allurement of liking" is both extended through and balanced or
checked by visual "contentation"; desire is created by extravagant
material display, but hand-in-hand come faculties of control and
temperance. Looking at Holdenby, Burghley's gaze is both pleasur-
able and moderated. His eyes are simultaneously delighted and
contained, as his "rational and moral faculties" remind him that
everything he views belongs to someone else.

I conclude my interpretation of this "simple" letter of appreciation by hinting at some of the negative energies that are inextricably
built into the "allurement of liking," and I will do so by reconsider-
ing Burghley's seemingly innocuous reference to Momus. The allusion to the Greek god of blame and mockery implicates Burghley
himself, even if the author's playful rhetoric desires to eschew such
an identification. Inasmuch as Burghley is a Momus unleashed during his self-guided tour of Holdenby, this allusion slyly, covertly
and most adroitly ushers criticism and envious blame into the visual
equation. As I have already argued, Holdenby intended to create
wonder and amazement in its visitors and viewers; it aimed "to allure liking." It also sought to control that "liking," insisting that the
viewer's gaze be restrained and tempered. The eye of the beholder
was thus harnessed both through an overwhelming display of material stuff (objects that indicated personal ownership, authority and
possession) and a deployment of successive thresholds which de-
marcated private as opposed to public space, common as opposed to
aristocratic ground, low versus high places. Such efforts to contain,
or at least moderate, the viewer's desire are far from absolute, however, and could easily fall short or fail altogether. Burghley's claim
that "truly a Momus could find no fault" with Hatton's house is not
a true measure of his reaction to Holdenby but rather a testament
to Cecil's abilities in the courtier-like arts of deception and decorously veiled flattery. Among the most architecturally informed patrons of his time,[21] and an intensely critical, even competitive man,

---

[19] *OED*, con. 1b.

[20] *OED*, con. 6.

[21] Cecil's knowledge of and interest in architecture are obvious. As one
of the primary followers of the Earl of Somerset in the early 1550s, his

Burghley, as Momus, surely found some matters worthy of his censure at Holdenby, a house that has always been viewed as derivative
of Burghley's own Theobalds.[22] In writing as a friend and co-
councilor, however, he sees no need to elaborate upon such faults.
He contains his envy, blame and castigation, but his playful admission of Momus (silenced though the god may be) into the letter
signals the existence or the possibility of such critical reactions. In
short, the "allurement of liking" purposed and effected by houses
like Holdenby and Theobalds was forever linked with the potentially negative energies of envy, jealousy, criticism, and various
kinds of iconoclasm, including the possible destruction or deface-
ment of material and the violation of thresholds.

---

enthusiasm for architecture can be anticipated. Not only did he fabricate
two of the era's largest country houses as well as an impressive town-house
on London's Strand, but he also exercised primary authority over the Office of the Royal Works and avidly collected books on architecture, perspective and fortifications. For the results of his education in Somerset's
circle, see Airs, 1975, 29, and in a more sympathetic light, Howard, 207.
For his influence on the Royal Works, see Howard Montagu Colvin, *The
History of the King's Works, 1485-1660*, vol. 3.1 (London: Her Majesty's
Stationery Office, 1975), 71-120; and John Summerson, *A Description of
Maps and Architectural Drawings in the Collection made by William
Cecil First Baron Burghley, now at Hatfield House* (Oxford: Roxburghe
Club, 1971), 79. On his acquisitions of architectural treatises and books,
see Lucy Gent, *Picture and Poetry, 1560-1620: Relations between Litera-
ture and the Visual Arts in the English Renaissance* (Leamington Spa:
James Hall, 1981), 66-86.

[22] Malcolm Airs has recently claimed, following Girouard's work on
Holdenby, that Hatton's estate probably did top Theobalds, not just in
size but in the cohesiveness of its program. Of the same letter under consideration here, Airs writes, playfully yet appropriately, that "[o]ne can
almost hear the noise of his gritted teeth when Burghley wrote to compliment Hatton on the 'allure' and 'magnificence' of Holdenby . . . Hatton
freely admitted his debt to Theobalds and his motive for building on such
a scale was the same as Burghley's: to provide an occasional palace for the
queen. It must have given Burghley immense satisfaction that not once
did she deign to visit that 'holy shrine' in the Midlands, preferring instead
the hospitality of her lord treasurer in the home counties." Airs, 2002, 8.
While I believe Airs overstates Theobalds' value as the queen's palace, I
find most apt his sense of the courtier-like competition between the two
men.

Tracing out both the construction of, and reactions to, allurement and contentation at the Elizabethan prodigy house requires much more space than this provisional article affords, even if such a study were to focus on a single house, such as Holdenby, Theobalds, or the Earl of Leicester's Kenilworth Castle. Here, I can but gesture at how such an investigation might unfold through a brief consideration of the remarks made by two men who lived and worked outside of Hatton and Burghley's privileged court milieu, but whose work necessitated incursions into such circles. Although their comments relate to Burghley's Theobalds, not Holdenby, their statements nevertheless manifest the centripetal pull of desire—allurement—and the centrifugal push away—contentation—that stems from someone else's propriety and ownership. Both of these authors are powerfully attracted by the charms of Burghley's Hertfordshire estate, but each author, too, discovers to some degree the necessity of disenchantment with, and disengagement from, Cecil's mansion. Like Cecil at Holdenby, they recognize, confront, and disarm their own internal Momus.

The first of these reports is an excerpt from John Norden's 1598 *Description of Hertfordshire*, a late Elizabethan chorography, or verbal mapping, of the county for which, intriguingly, the author was unable to gain the support and sponsorship of Burghley, who earlier in the reign had been a major patron of several mapping projects.[23] The second, more general testimony emerges from the dedication of John Gerard's *Herball* of 1597. Gerard was a significant Elizabethan botanist who served as Burghley's primary gardener, and in this capacity he traveled extensively on the continent in search of exotic plants, flowers and fruits that he might cultivate in Cecil's gardens.[24] Each of these texts, then, entails issues of Burghley's patronage, suggesting that we must read behind or beyond the overt praise the authors' distinct positions might seem to necessitate. Certainly their comments about Burghley's house and gardens are neither value free nor wholly objective, but this does not restrict their usefulness in our efforts to recover a sense of Burghley's em-

---

[23] See Richard Helgerson, *Forms of Nationhood: The Elizabethan Writing of England* (Chicago: Univ. of Chicago Press, 1992), 107-47.

[24] See Robert H. Jeffers, *The Friends of John Gerard, 1545-1612, Surgeon and Botanist* (Falls Village, CT, 1967).

ployment of the allurement of liking and the contentation of the eyes at Theobalds, as long as we read with an eye for nuance.

One other factor powerfully conjoins these two texts: they both emerge in the final years of Burghley's life (Burghley died in August 1598). Thus Norden's and Gerard's remarks derive from a liminal moment in the history of the estate and the family it inscribed and represented. As I have argued elsewhere, I am convinced that William Cecil built Theobalds first and foremost as the hereditary property of his dear second son and political heir, Robert. While the home grew—both physically and metaphorically—to encompass and embrace Queen Elizabeth, it always remained about, and intended for, Robert.[25] Such familial significations were carefully packed into the specifics of Theobalds' material and spatial deployment of the allurement of liking, and intentions of familial and dynastic transfer must have been especially apparent in 1597-1598, years that witnessed a steady decline in Burghley's health and a consequent increase in the amount of time Robert Cecil spent overseeing both the family's and the Queen's business.

Considering the size and opulence of Theobalds—it must have easily been the most impressive private domestic residence in the county, visibly and unmistakably impressing its huge footprint upon the land[26]—Norden's comments are surprisingly brief. He writes,

> [a] most stately house . . . [t]o speak of the state and beauty thereof as large as it deserveth, for curious buildings, delightful walkes, and pleasant conceites within and without, and other things very glorious and ellegant to be seene would challenge a great portion of this little

---

[25] See James M. Sutton, "The Decorative Program at Elizabethan Theobalds: Educating an Heir and Promoting a Dynasty," *Studies in the Decorative Arts: An International Journal* 7.1 (1999-2000): 33-64.

[26] Sir Thomas Smith's Hill Hall was 7 ½ miles distant, and Cecil's brother-in law, Anthony Cooke, kept house at Gidea Hall, 12 miles away. Another brother-in-law, Nicholas Bacon, began building Gorhambury one year prior to Burghley's commencement at Theobalds; this famous estate was 15 miles away. The area was also replete with royal palaces, including Enfield, Hertford Castle, Hatfield and Havering-at Bower, none further than 11 miles. See John Summerson, "The Building of Theobalds, 1564-1585," *Archaelogia* 97 (1959): 107.

> treatise, and therefore least I should come shorte of that
> due commendation that it deserveth, I leave it, as indeed
> it is, a princely seate.[27]

All the hallmarks of the allurement of liking can be found here, and
Norden feels too, though in his own manner, the effect of the contentation of the eyes. The passage is framed and contained by the
insistence that the house is "stately" and "princely." Such framing
apprehends immediately the ownership issues the place powerfully
projects, and subtly suggests, too, the dual nature of Theobalds. It
is both a "stately" aristocratic home, the place of the Cecils (who
remain unnamed, untouched, unappropriated here), and a "princely
seate," a palace literally (and symbolically) designed for the Queen
(who is also an unnamed but tangible presence in the passage). In
between these bookends decorously asserting property rights, delight and pleasure stream forth. Norden finds at Theobalds "curious
buildings, delightfull walkes, and pleasant conceits within and
without, and other things very glorious and ellegant." Clearly, his
liking has been allured: his pleasure is tangible, in fact, far more
tangible than the estate itself. For we have here not a very reliable
physical or spatial description of the place—we receive no indication of the relative position of things, nor their individual aspects—
but rather an emotional register of the experience of viewing. If
Norden's project is to make the land speak, to name and describe
those things the county called Hertfordshire presents to him, when
he arrives at Theobalds this program is singularly confounded and
partially muted.

Why does Norden find the description of Theobalds so difficult,
so beyond his abilities? On the surface of his text, he claims that it
is primarily a problem of size. He simply does not have enough
pages—or enough words, enough *copia*, for that matter—to adequately render the verbal mapping the place demands: "[t]o speak
of the state and beauty thereof as large as it deserveth . . . would
challenge a great portion of this little treatise." Certainly, this is in
its own manner a high compliment to Burghley, admitting as it
does the sheer bulk, the mass of material, that composes Theobalds. In the Elizabethan building code of the prodigy house, we

---

[27] John Norden, *Speculi Britaniae pass: A Description of Hertfordshire*
(1598), 34.

again see that overwhelming size matters. I believe, however, that
this text also shows powerfully the dual workings of the contentation of the eyes. Norden's experience is after all primarily visual, as
he admits when he says these "other things . . . [are] to be seene."
As I said, the pleasure he takes in viewing is tangible (tactile and
even material), but also palpable is the co-extensive chastisement of
the eye. Size is the external, admitted excuse for his failure to describe; the moral and rational knowledge that the grandeur that he
sees is not his, and the consequent acquiescence and acceptance of
this situation, represents a more illusive reason for his brevity.[28] To
verbally map a place like Theobalds is not to own it, nor appropriate it: only Burghley, or his son, or the prince upon certain occasions, could make that claim. Inasmuch as the sheer massiveness of
the place overwhelms Norden's descriptive faculties, so too does the
restraining operation of the allurement of liking induce him to
"leave it" just as soon as he arrives, "least I should come shorte of
that due commendation that it deserveth."

Norden writes directly about Theobalds, and indirectly, covertly,
addresses Burghley, who had refused him patronage. Gerard, on
the other hand, in dedicating his *Herball* to Cecil, addresses a long-
standing patron directly and comments upon the estate in passing.
Despite its modal and generic differences, however, Gerard's dedication also reveals the operation of the allurement of liking, if in a
specifically horticultural rather than architectural vein. He begins
by speaking of the pleasures of the garden through an allusion to
other material, visual arts of the period:

> [i]f delight may provoke mens labor, what greater de-
> light is there than to behold the earth apparelled with
> plants, as with a robe of embroidered worke, set with
> Orient pearles and garnished with great diversitie of rare
> and costly jewels. If this varietie and perfection of col-
> ours may affect the eie, it is such in herbs and floures,
> that no *Apelles*, no *Zeuxis* ever could by any art expresse
> the like . . . But these delights are in the outward senses:
> the principal delight is in the mind, singularly enriched

---

[28] We should recall, in this regard, the fact that Cecil had refused to
patronize Norden's project. In part, then, the map-maker might refuse to
speak at greater length about Theobalds because he comes so near the
great patron's wrath at this very moment.

with the knowledge of these visible things . . . to speake
again in a word of delight, gardens, especially such as
your Honor hath, furnished with many rare simples, do
singularly delight, when in them a man doth behold a
flourishing shew of summer beauties in the midst of
Winters force, and a goodly Spring of flours, when
abroad a leafe is not to be seene.[29]

Despite the necessary caveats that must attend all dedications in
this period, I believe we can, and indeed should, assume that
Gerard is in some sense speaking for Burghley here, offering us, as
the patron's mouthpiece, a philosophy and aesthetics of flowers to
which they both strongly subscribe.[30] In short, if we wish to know
how Burghley thought a garden might work to allure liking, if we
want to know how or in what manner the several gardens at Theobalds might have aimed to produce too the contentation of the

---

[29] John Gerard, *The Herball or Generall Historie of Plantes* (London,
1636), 4. I wish to thank the librarians and staff of Worcester College,
Oxford, who kindly allowed me to work with their early edition of
Gerard's treatise.

[30] Later in his dedication, Gerard in fact forwards this claim of near
equivalence between him and his patron in horticultural matters. In the
garden, they truly are of like mind and mutual spirit. Such an insistence,
seemingly dangerous for an author to make in this period, here seems
grounded upon a long and close working relationship between the two
men. Gerard claims "that which sometimes was the study of great Phy-
losophers and mightie Princes, is now neglected, except it be of some few,
whose spirit and wisdome hath carried them among other parts of wisdome and counsell, to a care and study of speciall herbes, both for the fur-
nishing of their gardens, and furthermore of their knowledge: among
whom I may justly affirme and publish your Honor to be one . . . for under your Lordship I have served . . . now by the space of twenty yeares . . .
I have added from forreine places all the varietie of herbes and floures that
I might any way obtaine . . . so they might live and prosper under our
clymat, as in their native and proper countrey: what my successe hath
beene . . . I leave to the report of they that hath seene your Lordships gardens." Gerard, 5.

eyes, we cannot do better than to pay some considerable attention to this passage from Gerard's dedication.[31]

Burghley's gardener begins with an insistence upon the potential efficacy and worth of "delight," suggesting that such an emotion or sensation is not an end in and of itself, but something which, properly understood, "provokes labor." Indeed, says Gerard, "delight" can be provocative, but not only in the morally pejorative manner a puritan ethos (or even a seriously considered religious ethos such as Burghley espoused) might have trained us to expect. The gardener squarely situates his theory of pleasure in a viewing of the natural world, inquiring "what greater delight is there than to behold the earth apparelled with plants?" While God remains unnamed here, we can infer that for both Gerard and Cecil, the divine presence authors this artfully pleasing natural world.

Within this formulation, posed as an easily answered question, there lies hidden two more difficult queries. That the earth is delightful, and that taking pleasure in this beauty is morally and religiously acceptable: these are easily agreed upon propositions. How are we rightly to "behold" this beauty? And how do we correctly "labor," what do we do, in response to such delight? Gerard begins to answer the question of sight by analogies to the world of costume and ornamentation, and completes his response via a fascinating *paragone* that opposes classical norms of painting to contemporary modes of native gardening. He then moves on to construe a solution to the second issue, suggesting some fifty-five years before Marvell that, having viewed God's garden, man should go on to create a new, fresh garden where the mind can "annihiliat[e] all that's made / To a green thought in a green shade," and the soul, bird-like, can take flight "into the boughs," where "till prepared for longer flight" it might "wave in its plumes the various light."[32]

Gerard's comparison of the earth's apparel to human costume cannot be overlooked, for in glancing at Elizabethan fashion, he

---

[31] For further commentary on the decided enthusiasm for gardening held by both Burghley and Robert Cecil, see Paula Henderson, "A Shared Passion: The Cecils and Their Gardens," in Croft, 99-120.

[32] Andrew Marvell, "The Garden" 47-8, 52, 55-6. Quoted from *The Norton Anthology of English Literature,* 7th edition (New York: W. W. Norton and Co., 2000), 1699-1700.

encodes valuable information about how gardens might allure liking. If Janet Arnold, Gloria Kury, Ann Rosalind Jones and Peter
Stallybrass, and Jane Scheider have furthered our understanding of
the materiality and emphasis upon surface decoration and ornamentation in Elizabethan dress,[33] we can in turn use their insights
to unpack Gerard's assertion that the planted earth is akin to "a
robe of embroidered worke, set with Orient pearles and garnished
with great diversitie of rare and costly jewels." Here we find the
same loving interest in texture and weave, precious objects, gleam-
ing gems and "glancing surfaces," that these scholars have found
encoded within the period's fashion system. Furthermore, just as
this clothing system relies upon the play of light along and off its
multi-colored, variegated surfaces, so too does Gerard's bejeweled
earth await illumination in order to achieve its full effects. Gloria
Kury, likening the intended display of George Clifford's Elizabethan armour to the fetishized objects displayed in modern high-
street shop windows (following Walter Benjamin, she claims the
armor as an Elizabethan example of the "wish image"), has contended that such

> objects are positioned so that their front surface is
> aligned with a picture plane; lighting is treated as a filter
> that enhances alluring properties while minimizing any
> considered unattractive. The result of these techniques is
> almost always a visual spectacle which features an object
> freed of physical weight and dependent on light and col-
> our for visibility . . . the goods in a wish image exist in
> two dimensions and gain in potency by doing so.[34]

I believe that Gerard pictures the ideal garden in the same manner:
as a two-dimensional surface of incredible texture and chromatic
pattern, appreciated fully only by an eye that comprehends and participates feelingly in its incredible diversity. Following his reference

---

[33] See Janet Arnold, *Patterns of Fashion: The Cut and Construction of
Clothes for Men and Women c. 1560-1620* (London: Macmillan, 1985);
Arnold, *Queen Elizabeth's Wardrobe Unlock'd* (Leeds: W. S. Maney &
Son Ltd., 1988); Kury, 404-14; Jones and Stallybrass, 1-85; and Jane
Schneider, "Fantastical Colors in Foggy London: The New Fashion Po-
tential of the Late Sixteenth Century" in Cowen Orlin, 109-27.

[34] Kury, 409-10.

to bejeweled clothes, he insists, "if this varietie and perfection of colours may affect the eie, it is in such herbs and floures." The gaze illuminates the artful garden, but only if the eye is open to, and comprehends, the patterned planes of (plant) material that compose it.

For Gerard, these garden planes, viewed correctly, are like, but go well beyond, painting, for "no Apelles, no Zeuxis ever could by any art expresse the like." The gardener casts off these heroic Greek artists as representative of notions of depiction he finds wanting: an eye that privileges naturalism, realism and optic perspective will not get very far in Gerard's garden of delights. Inasmuch as his ideal plot of earth is like a painting style, indeed that floral mode of depiction would have to be northern, if not Elizabethan: planar, patterned, paratactic, a canvas of soil that displays and celebrates the variegated colors upon its surface, a canvas where excess materiality trumps intellectualized design.[35]

Thus the eye beholding Gerard or Burghley's garden should delight, if not revel, in tactile stimulation. Such visual sensation, however, is outward looking; it should be accompanied by an inward and "principal delight" located "in the mind, singularly enriched with the knowledge of these visible things." In Burghley's garden, the eye of the beholder should delight both outwardly and inwardly; such interior mental pleasure has its own codes and restrictions, but most fundamentally, the turn inward is (Burghley and his

---

[35] Gerard's emphases on the color effects provided by gardens become all the more interesting in light of Schneider's recent claims that during the late Elizabethan years, black and white clothing was strongly preferred over colored robes, whose dyes derived by and large from the importation of foreign materials. She writes that, following the Queen's lead, "the court as a whole seemed to shun the competitive display of variegated colors as a route to prestige or status. Drawn to this court as if by a magnet and forced to maintain expensive residences and rounds of hospitality in London, members of the aristocracy and gentry certainly spent prodigious amounts of their family fortunes on clothing. But the most invidious displays of fashion had little or no chromatic resonance: starched ruffs, lace or pearled embroidery, and fantastic shapes. Compared with color, each of these elements depended heavily, if not utterly, on native, as opposed to foreign, craft production." Schneider, 115. Thus, the thoroughly native, natural colors of the flowers and plants Gerard promotes and plants in Burghley's garden trump not only painting, but the fashion system as well.

agent Gerard hope) a turn away from appropriation and envy. The eye that only takes pleasure in outward beauty is in danger of breaking into outwardly-directed iconoclasm; such a beholder might pick a few flowers, carve his initials upon a tree, or swat at the honeybee buzzing about his head. But the beholder who does as Gerard directs, turning to inward contemplation, will not damage or ruin the outward garden; just as the poet-speaker in Marvell's garden retreats into a philosophical and theological green world, so too the flights of fancy taken by the mind and soul of Gerard's ideal viewer are intended to be re-creative and uplifting. This sort of garden-induced poetic reverie precisely describes where Gerard's dedication to Burghley concludes. Repeating the word "delight" twice more, Gerard insists that "gardens, especially such as your Honor hath . . . do singularly delight, when in them a man do behold a flourishing shew of summer beauties in the midst of Winters force, and a goodly Spring of flours, when abroad a leafe is not to be seene." The theatre of Burghley's garden produces, for those who see it rightly, a masque of the four seasons, where through man's ingenuity summer forever conquers winter and spring trumps fall. To be allured into liking within Burghley's garden, argues Gerard, is to be issued into an ever-green place, a semi-miraculous second Eden. For the visitor who fully and "correctly" comprehends the contentation of the eyes, Burghley's plot might be a site of true self-renewal and recreation.

Despite the equivocal testimony of Norden's excerpt, and despite Gerard's neat and amenable dedication with its conciliatory, congratulatory conclusion, the question remains: just how far-reaching and how powerful were the dual claims of allurement and contentation at houses such as Theobalds, Holdenby, and Kenilworth? What alternative visions were possible to men and women who were excluded from these realms, and what price was paid, if any, by those who enjoyed the allurement but refused the contentation, who entered but in some manner never departed? I conclude by posing these questions; elsewhere I hope to begin to address them.

Florida International University

Discovering Authorial Intention in the Manuscript Sequences of Donne's Holy Sonnets

GARY A. STRINGER

HAVING previously published volumes on the funeral poems, the epigrams and epithalamions, and the love elegies,[1] the editors of *The Variorum Edition of the Poetry
of John Donne* will shortly submit to the press our volume on
Donne's Holy Sonnets. Our analysis of the manuscripts of these
poems has resulted in incontestable bibliographical evidence not
only that Donne intended his Holy Sonnets as a sequence—an idea
carrying important interpretive implications—but also that his conception of the sequence changed over time, leading him to revise
the texts of individual poems and to effect a major restructuring of
the overall arrangement.[2] To validate these claims and to clarify the
confused editorial history of the Holy Sonnets from the early seventeenth century onward will be the primary business of the remainder of this essay, though I will conclude with some remarks on the
problem of distinguishing authorial from second-party changes in
scribal manuscripts.

---

[1] *The Anniversaries and the Epicedes and Obsequies*, 1995; *The Epigrams, Epithalmions, Epitaphs, Inscriptions, and Miscellaneous Poems*,
1995; *The Elegies*, 2000—vols. 6, 8, and 2, respectively, of *The Variorum
Edition of the Poetry of John Donne* (Bloomington: Indiana Univ. Press,
1995-).

[2] Donne's epigrams reflect a similar pattern of revision—see the *Donne
Variorum* 8: 5-27 and passim. Revision of individual poems occurs within
the epithalamions and several of the elegies, as is shown in vols. 8 and 2,
respectively, of the *Variorum*.

Before proceeding to these matters, however, I should like briefly to rehearse the textual circumstances that a Donne scholar faces. Over the course of his life, Donne wrote about 200 poems numbering *in toto* close to 9800 lines. With the exceptions of the Anniversaries—the long commendatory poems on the death of Elizabeth Drury—and a scattering of shorter pieces, however, Donne "published" his poems only in manuscript, circulating copies among members of a coterie of friends, patrons, and prospective patrons, who in turn circulated them to others. The first collected edition of Donne's poetry, the 1633 *POEMS*, set into type from non-authorial manuscripts, was not published until two years after the author's death, and virtually no Donne holographs survive: of poetic materials in the poet's own hand, we have only four brief inscriptions, a Latin epitaph on his wife, and the sixty-three-line verse epistle "To the Lady Carey and Mrs Essex Riche." The remaining scribal copies of Donne's poems, however, total about 5,000 exempla in 243 different manuscripts, and many poems survive in over 50 separate copies. From these materials and whatever may be gleaned from the four-centuries-long editorial tradition, the modern editor must construct a text; and the goal of the *Variorum*, ideally stated, is to recover and present what Donne actually wrote. This always-difficult task, as I will demonstrate here, is considerably complicated by the survival of multiple authentic versions of poems and groups of poems among the early artifacts.

Compared to the Elegies, for which it was necessary to analyze 823 transcriptions totaling 48,656 lines of data, the Holy Sonnets pose a considerably easier editorial problem (see Figure 1 for a list of short forms and sigla used below). As Figure 2 shows, 196 copies of Donne's nineteen Holy Sonnets remain in the manuscript record, and five of these—those in AF1 and B6—derive from print. Drawing on the two manuscripts from which he derived most of his material (see Figure 3), the editor of the 1633 *POEMS* (siglum A) presented in a numbered sequence their shared set of twelve Holy Sonnets, beginning with "As due by many titles" and concluding with "Father, part of his double interest." In the 1635 edition two years later, however, he interpolated four additional poems from yet a third source, and this editorially confected sequence of sixteen Holy Sonnets passed on not only into the remaining five seventeenth-century editions/issues of the *POEMS* (C-G), but also (see Figure 4)—with the single exception of Alford (1839)—into every edition of the eighteenth and nineteenth centuries, including those of Tonson (1719), Bell (1779), Anderson (1793), Chalmers (1810), Lowell (1855), Grosart (1872-73), the Grolier editor (1895), and Chambers (1896).[3] And since his examination of the manuscripts failed to yield "a definite significance in any order" (II:231), even Grierson (1912)[4] reproduced the customary sequence of *1635*, appending as items seventeen through nineteen "Since she whom I loved," "Show me dear Christ," and "O to vex me," which had been discovered in the Westmoreland manuscript in the 1890s.[5] Grierson's procedure was then imitated exactly by his immediate successors Hayward (1929) and Bennett (1942). In 1952, however, persuaded that only the twelve-poem set of *1633* embodied Donne's intentions for the sequence, Helen Gardner restored

---

[3] Jacob Tonson, *Poems on Several Occasions* . . . (London, 1719); John Bell, *The Poetical Works of Dr. John Donne* . . . (London, 1779); Robert Anderson, *The Poetical Works of Dr. John Donne* . . . (London and Edinborough, 1793); Alexander Chalmers, *The Poems of John Donne* (London, 1810); Henry Alford, *The Works of John Donne, D. D.* . . . (London, 1839); James Russell Lowell, *The Poetical Works of Dr. John Donne* . . . (Boston, 1855); Alexander B. Grosart, *The Complete Poems of John Donne, D.D.* . . . (privately printed [London], 1872-73); James Russell Lowell [C. E. Norton and Mabel Burnett], *The Poems of John Donne* (New York: The Grolier Club, 1895); and E. K. Chambers, *The Poems of John Donne* (London, 1896).

[4] Herbert J. C. Grierson, *The Poems of John Donne*, 2 vols. (Oxford: Clarendon Press, 1912). Subsequent twentieth-century editions include John Hayward, *John Donne, Dean of St. Paul's: Complete Poetry and Selected Prose* (Bloomsbury: Nonesuch Press, 1929); Roger D. Bennett, *The Complete Poems of John Donne* (Chicago: Packard and Co., 1942); Helen Gardner, *John Donne: The Divine Poems* (Oxford: Clarendon Press, 1952; 2nd. ed., 1978); John T. Shawcross, *The Complete Poetry of John Donne* (New York: Doubleday, 1967); A. J. Smith, *John Donne: The Complete English Poems* (Harmondsworth and Baltimore: Penguin, 1971); and C. A. Patrides, *The Complete English Poems of John Donne* (London: Dent, 1985).

[5] Edmund Gosse owned the Westmoreland ms. in the 1890s and from it had published *HSShe* singly in *The Jacobean Poets* (London, 1894) and then *HSShe*, *HSShow*, and *HSVex* as part of his presentation of the entire Westmoreland sequence in *The Life and Letters of John Donne*, 2 vols. (London, 1899).

its order, printing as a numbered series the four "Sonnets added in 1635" and characterizing them in her introduction as "penitential," a thematically unified set on "sin and tears for sin" (xli). And she justified her reordering of "Oh might those sighs" and "I am a little world" as an effort to present this theme more effectively. Finally, she concluded her section of Holy Sonnets with the Westmoreland poems separately numbered in a three-item series. In his edition fifteen years later, Shawcross (1967) adopted Gardner's ordering of the poems exactly (including the rearrangement of "Oh might those sighs" and "I am a little world"), though he numbered all nineteen poems in a continuous series. Most recently, Smith (1971) and Patrides (1985), obviously unpersuaded by Gardner, reverted to the order of *1635*, continuing on the path blazed by Grierson.

A half century after Gardner troubled the waters, as the discussion above makes clear, there is still no consensus on the question of what order Donne intended for the Holy Sonnets. Given the critical implications of the issue, however, a definitive answer is much to be desired. Fortunately, we are now able to settle this matter bibliographically by describing the transmissional history through which these poems evolved before ever making their way into print. As Figure 5 shows, Donne's first collection of religious sonnets is that preserved in B46, H5, HH1, and the C9-H6 pair—five artifacts constituting for these poems the traditional Group III as first described by Grierson in 1912. Headed "Diuine Meditations," these are presented in this family of artifacts as a numbered sequence of twelve that begins with "Thou hast made me" and concludes with "Wilt thou love God as he thee?" Bearing the revised heading "Holy Sonnets," this Group-III sequence next appears at the head of the numbered series of nineteen poems in NY3, the lone Group-IV manuscript, and to it have been added "Spit in my face," "Why are we by all creatures waited on," "What if this present were the world's last night," and "Batter my heart," as well as "Since she whom I loved," "Show me dear Christ," and "O to vex me." The Group-I and Group-II mss. listed to the right of NY3 in Figure 5 revert to a twelve-poem sequence of Holy Sonnets that incorporates eight of the Group-III poems, but discards the first, third, seventh, and tenth ("Thou has made me," "Oh might those sighs," "I am a little world," and "If faithful souls"), moves "Father part of his double interest" to the concluding position at the very end of the sequence, and inserts "Spit in my face," "Why are we by all creatures," "What if this present," and "Batter my heart" into positions seven through ten of the new arrangement. This differently constituted and reorganized sequence is that which enters print in 1633, set into type primarily from a Group-I manuscript. Two years later, as we noted above (see Figure 3), B's editor reclaims from a Group-III manuscript the previously dropped "Thou has made me," "O might those sighs," "I am a little world," and "If faithful souls"; and this expanded collection of sixteen poems defined the genre until Edmund Gosse added the final three from NY3 in the late nineteenth century.

Each of the manuscript groups identified above, of course, is defined as a group by distinctive features, including verbal variants, that are unique to its members. Among these variants are a number, dispersed across the spectrum of groups, that cannot reasonably be attributed to scribal error or the general entropy of the transmissional system and must therefore reflect authorial revision (some guidelines for distinguishing authorial from scribal changes will be presented below). A few representative examples will suffice to make the point. Revisions that Donne made of the early/Group-III text before it passed into the hands of the NY3 scribe (see Figure 6) include the alteration of "shall see" to "do see" in "As due by many titles" 12; "thy last will" to "that last will" in "Father, part of his double interest" 14; "o Lord" to "o God" in "I am a little world" 13; "Thy griefe, for he put it into my brest" to "Thy true griefe, for he put it in my brest" in "If faithful souls" 14; and "Rest of their bodyes" to "Rest of their bones" in "Death be not proud" 8.

As the NY3 text migrated to the subsequent stage of development in Group I, moreover, Donne not only reorganized the original twelve-item sequence, as noted above, but also made further changes in the wording of the poems. Among the 8 original poems that he retained in this reorganization, for instance (see Figure 7), we find the change of "and quicken" to "again" in "Father, part of his double interest" 12 and of "Or as a Theife" to "Or like a Theife" in "O my black soul" 5. And the texts of three of the four replacement sonnets also undergo substantive revision before showing up in the Group-I sequence (see Figure 8): NY3's version of "Spit in my face" 3-4 changes from "For I haue sin'd, and sin'd: and humbly hee / Which could do no iniquity hath dyde" to "For I haue sin'd,

and sin'd: and only hee / Who could do no iniquity hath dyde";
NY3's "Why ame I by all Creatures wayted on?" becomes "Why are
wee by all Creatures wayted on?" and in line 9 of that same sonnet
NY3's "Alas I'ame weaker, wo'is me" changes to "Weaker I am,
woe is me"; and NY3's "prayed forgiuenes for his foes ranck spight"
in "What if this present" 8 is altered to "prayed forgiuenes for his
foes fierce spight." Finally, we must note one last authorial change
that appears in the Group-II text. As shown in Figure 9, this revision appears in line 7 of "This is my play's last scene," where Donne
alters "Or presentlye, I knowe not, see that face" to "But my euer
waking part shall see that face," effecting a major ideological shift
that Gardner used to anchor a theory of dating these poems (see
Gardner, xliii-l).

Considerable intrinsic interest attaches to many of these individual changes, of course, but the possibility of tracing the author's
hand through successive stages of revision carries a much broader
significance: since each of these revisions subsists in the context not
only of the individual poem, but also of a group of poems, the very
fact of their existence necessarily implies Donne's conscious decision either to maintain or to modify the organization of the larger
unit at given points in time. That he retains the Group-III order in
revising the text for NY3/Group IV, therefore, validates the authenticity of the Group-III arrangement, while his maintenance of
the Group-I order as he effects the Group-II revisions both confirms his continued endorsement of that arrangement and shows
that the structural changes introduced in the transition from the
NY3 sequence to that in Group I are deliberate. We may thus be
confident that at various points in the life of the work, Donne intended both the early, Group-III arrangement and the later,
Groups-I-and-II sequence; and each of these is a necessary object
of study for anyone seriously interested in Donne's Holy Sonnets.
Our volume will present both, and we expect it to generate a great
deal of new criticism not only on the previously unprinted early sequence, but also on the later arrangement—which, though it has
sometimes been treated as a sequence, has never been so explicated
in a reading grounded in solid bibliographical fact.[6]

---

[6] Though her understanding of the relationship between the Group-I
and Group-II arrangement and that in Group III is erroneous, Gardner
correctly avers that the twelve-sonnet set in groups I and II is authorially

* * * * *

Finding the needle of authorial revision in the haystack of variation that arose as Donne's poems passed from copyist to copyist in
a manuscript culture is a tricky business, and the editor who claims
to have succeeded in this task may well be regarded with skepticism. Indeed, the very idea that such a needle exists is by no means
commonplace among Donne scholars, not only because we lack the
holograph artifacts that might provide ocular proof, but also because in one of the more widely known references that he makes to
his role as a poet—the letter to Henry Goodyere of 20 December
1614—Donne depicts himself as one who tended to write a poem,
present it to the intended audience, and be done with it.[7] As I have
suggested above with respect to the Holy Sonnets, however (and as
we have shown with respect to other poems in previous volumes of
the *Variorum*), abundant manuscript evidence counters this portrait
of Donne as a neglectful custodian of his own work, revealing instead an artist who very much cared about his poems and who continued to fine-tune or revise individual items, sometimes in
multiple stages, even after distributing the original versions. The

---

sanctioned; and she briefly suggests that it embodies Donne's intention to
"creat[e] a balance of six against six . . . " (xliii). In a trenchant analysis of
Gardner's confused account of the Group-III arrangement, Patrick F.
O'Connell, "The Successive Arrangements of Donne's 'Holy Sonnets,'"
PQ 60, no. 3 (Summer 1981), 323-42, is the first to suggest that the
Group-III arrangement also "has Donne's authority behind it" (329).
O'Connell also advances bibliographical reasons for viewing Westmore-
land's Holy Sonnets as a set of twelve, a set of four, and a set of three
rather than as a distinct, nineteen-item authorial sequence; I agree with
his conclusion, though not with his account of how the Westmoreland
came to exist in its present form. Among the few who have interpreted the
Group-I and -II arrangement as a sequence is Carol Sicherman, "Donne's
Discoveries," *SEL* 11 (1971), 69-88.

   [7] In the letter Donne says he is "brought to a necessity of printing . . .
[his] Poems" and speaks of needing to retrieve copies of some of them
from Goodyere's "old book," averring that it has "cost . . . [him] more de-
ligence to seek [his poems] . . . , than it did to make them" (*Letters to
Severall Persons of Honour*, ed. M. Thomas Hester [New York: Scholar's
Facsimiles, 1977], pp. 196-7).

question is, How do we discriminate such instances of change from those that are merely adventitious?

In working with the Donne materials over the years, I have developed a set of four criteria in terms of which to evaluate a given variant's claim to authenticity. The questions to be asked are these:

(a) Does the reading represent a "genuine alternative"?[8] A positive answer to this question entails the judgment that the variant in question cannot be dismissed as a scribal effort at improvement or clarification (i.e., "sophistication" or "trivialization") and that its aptness of sound and/or sense is essentially equivalent to that of the alternative.

(b) Is the reading readily explicable as a scribal misreading or slip of the pen? Application of this rubric requires familiarity with the diversity of forms, some of them quite idiosyncratic, found in the hand-writing of Elizabethan copyists.

(c) Is the reading appropriately located in the poem's transmissional history? Generally speaking, only a position at the head of a line of transmission, where scribal corruptions are least likely to appear, qualifies as "appropriate" under this rubric. To ascertain whether a variant is so placed, of course, requires development of a stemma or schema of the relationships among a poem's various sources, and the failure to carry out such filiation will doom one's efforts to separate authorial from scribal changes.

(d) Are there extrinsic considerations touching individual scribes, artifacts, or transcriptions that affect confidence in the legitimacy of particular readings? With the exception of Rowland Woodward (who penned the Westmoreland manuscript [NY3]) and a couple of others, the personal identity of Donne's copyists is unknown and thus speaks neither for nor against the likelihood of their accuracy. In working through (especially) the major manuscript collections of Donne's poetry, however, even though their scribes remain anonymous, one eventually acquires a general sense of the reliability of each and can bring that experience to bear in evaluating specific readings.

In practice, the answer to any one of these guiding questions may be far from clear-cut, and they may thus not lead to certainty

---

[8] The phrase is Gardner's (p. 124), used to describe certain powerfully appealing readings that she is not willing to set down as "revisions."

in every particular instance. Collectively, however, they provide a means of minimizing the element of subjective taste in the task of discrimination and put the enterprise upon a systematic, if not quite scientific, footing. Any variant that passes muster with all of these questions is quite likely authorial, and the case is virtually airtight if the change is incorporated into a subsequent stage of development that itself exhibits further revision. In what follows I will discuss the applicability of these criteria to some of the instances of revision cited above, and I will conclude by examining an example among the Holy Sonnets that shows the limitations of their usefulness.

Figure 6, for example, displays five changes that NY3 introduces into the earlier, Group-III text, and all qualify as authorial by the above-listed criteria. The alterations in *HSLittle* 13 (of "o Lord" to "o God") and *HSSouls* 14 (of "griefe . . . into" to "true griefe . . . in") are not validated by their carry-over into the later Group-I and -II text (these sonnets are among those omitted from the revised sequence); but both represent genuine alternatives and neither is a mere blunder. The same may be said of the alterations in *HSDue* 12 (of "shall" to "do"), *HSPart* 14 (of "thy" to "that"), and *HSDeath* 8 (of "bodyes" to "bones") (though the case for "shall/do" and "thy/that" is perhaps somewhat less clear), and—more importantly—all these changes persist in the text of the later sequence, a fact putting their legitimacy beyond reasonable doubt. And the case for the authenticity of these variations is further enhanced not only by the presence of another twelve or thirteen Group-III-to-NY3 changes for which similarly strong arguments can be made, but also by the kind of extrinsic authority mentioned in rubric "d" above: NY3 is in the hand of Rowland Woodward, friend and exchanger of youthful verses with Donne and sometime secretary to the first Earl of Westmoreland. All our work with this manuscript to date reveals Woodward as a highly accurate, noninterventionist transcriber of Donne's poems and suggests that the copies from which he worked derived more or less immediately from the poet's own papers. There is thus every reason to attribute NY3's text of the Holy Sonnets—including variants in which it differs from both earlier and later versions—to Donne himself. Similar arguments can be marshaled to defend the judgments reflected in figures 8 and 9.

A crux I have not listed among Donne's revisions of the Holy Sonnets, one showing that even the application of the criteria cited above cannot in every instance eliminate the necessity of interpretive judgment, appears in line 13 of "If poisonous Mineralls." The early/ Group-III text reads as follows:

> yf poysonous Mineralls, or yf the Tree
>   whose fruite threwe death on (els immortall) vs,
>   yf letcherous Goates, yf serpents envious
> Cannott be damnd', alas, why should I be?
> why should intent and reason borne in me,
>   make sinnes (els equall) in me more haynous?
>   and mercy being easy and glorious
> To God, in his sterne wrath why threatens he?
> but who am I, that dare dispute with thee?
>   O God, o of thy only worthy bloud
>   and my teares make a heav'nly Lethean floud
> and drowne in it my sinnes blacke memory
>   that thou remember them **no more** as debt,
>   I thincke it mercy, yf thou wilt forgett.

The later NY3 and groups I and II, however, read the sestet the way we are used to seeing it:

> But who am I that dare dispute with thee
>   O God? O of thyne only worthy blood
>   And my teares make a heauenly Lethean flood
> And drowne in it, my Sins blacke memoree.
>   That thou remember them, **Some clayme** as dett
>   I thinke it Mercy if thou wilt forgett.

There is no doubt that the chronology of change is as here shown: the "no more as debt" reading comes before "some clayme." But the question of whether "no more as debt" is an early authorial reading or a scribal corruption is harder. Since it appears in every member of Group III and since none of them was copied from any of the others, "no more" obviously existed in the urtext that stands at the head of this line of transmission (in other words, it cannot be discounted as an isolated mutation that crops us somewhere far down the family tree). Further, since no one is likely to have misread "some clayme" as "no more," this variant does not likely result from a scribal blunder. We are thus left with a logico-esthetic—rather than a purely bibliographical—question: do these variants represent genuine alternatives?

When I first began to consider this problem, I polled a number of colleagues on whether they thought "no more as debt" could have been Donne's initial reading in line 13. The responses ranged from a terse "No way!" to a lengthy scholarly disquisition ending with a cautiously worded " . . . yes, I think Donne may have written the 'no more' version. And I just might think it's the better version to boot." Before I reveal my opinion, I should point out that, fortunately, not everything rides on this answer. Since the *Variorum* will print multiple sequences, we do not have to choose only one of these alternatives. What is at stake is merely how we try to explain what has happened in this line.

With due respect to all my respondents who took the other side, I do not finally believe Donne wrote "remember them no more as debt." I base this judgment on a couple of primary points. First, that this variant appears in five extant witnesses is not necessarily significant, since all five could well descend from a scribal prototype into which this error had been introduced rather than from the author's holograph, and that lost urtext need not be more than one step removed from Donne's papers. Second, even though the replacement of "some clayme" with "no more" cannot be explained as a scribal misreading, it can readily be explained as a scribal trivialization.

Like many of Donne's, the construction involving "That thou remember them some clayme as debt" is both syntactically and conceptually difficult. By contrast, the construction involving "That thou remember them no more as debt" is syntactically easier, and it echoes a Biblical phrase that in Western, Biblical culture is virtually self-inscribing: "And their sinnes and iniquities will I remember no more" (Hebrews 10.17 and 8.12). (Americans may have noticed the iteration of this formula in the prayer of benediction at George W. Bush's inauguration.) If the scribe of the Group-III progenitor received a copy reading "some clayme as debt" and had trouble understanding the line, I can well imagine that he (or she) might have substituted a familiar phrase that seemed to make sense; and exercising such license would have been especially easy if that scribe knew he was not copying Donne's holograph directly (and thus felt less compunction about altering what he was looking at) and if the text he was looking at had no punctuation at the end of line 12.

All this conjecture, of course, may just be my way of ridding Donne of what I regard as an inferior line. So, in addition to its utter predictability, let me offer the brief outline of a further argument against the legitimacy of "remember them no more." Measured against the later "some clayme," the principal effect of the "no more" reading is, of course, to shift the referent of the pronoun "them" from the "some [people]" who claim God is obligated to remember them to "sins." "That thou remember my sins no more as debt" then becomes the meaning of line 13 in the Group-III text. This redefinition of the pronoun has at least the following three effects:

First, it links line 13 to line 12 in a relationship of cause and effect: "drowne in it my sinnes blacke memory / [So] that thou remember them no more as debt." And this connection consequently detaches line 13 syntactically from line 14, leaving "I think it mercy if thou wilt forget" to stand as a single-line conclusion in a way not otherwise found among Donne's sonnets. All the others, including those in *La Corona*, end with a final thought that stretches over at least a couplet. In structural terms, "no more as debt" thus renders this sonnet unique in Donne's practice.

Second, the syntactical realignment entailed in "no more as debt" drains the sestet of this poem of conceptual complexity and density. One of the respondents whom I polled noted that the reading runs the risk of making line 14 seem redundant, since "in a paraphrase, it might be made to say just what the preceding lines have already said." Indeed, it seems to me that line 12's "drowne . . . my Sinnes . . . memorie," line 13's "remember them no more," and line 14's "forget [them]" all do say substantially the same thing. Even though some new ideological freight is introduced by the concepts of "debt" in line 13 and "mercy" in line 14, I do not think the conclusion of the sonnet has near the specific gravity that we normally see in Donne and that the "some clayme" version has.

Finally, if "Some clayme as dett" were a revision of "no more as debt," it would represent a categorically different kind of change from any of those we have discussed above or of which I am otherwise aware in Donne's practice. In the examples I have surveyed, Donne changes individual words in order to adjust a concept or an image; or he rearranges the sequence, investing individual poems with different shades of meaning that arise from their altered position within the larger structure. But the transformation effected by this alteration is of a different logical order: the change of a mere two little words significantly alters the poem's syntax and its particular manner of embodying the sonnet form. And it simultaneously changes the denotative content of a number of words. In the last analysis, as highly as I regard Donne's wit and as strongly as I believe that if anyone could have hit on such a miraculously transformative emendation, he could have, that this is his revision of an originally lame passage seems less likely than that the lameness is the accidental by-product of a scribe's ignorant corruption of one of Donne's typically brilliant endings.

University of Southern Mississippi

Figure 1: Short Forms for Donne's Holy Sonnets

HSBatter	"Batter my heart"
HSBlack	"O my black soul"
HSDeath	"Death be not proud"
HSDue	"As due by many titles"
HSLittle	"I am a little world"
HSMade	"Thou has made me"
HSMin	"If poisonous minerals"
HSPart	"Father part of his double interest"
HSRound	"At the round earth's imagined corners"
HSScene	"This is my play's last scene"
HSShe	"Since she whom I loved"
HSShow	"Show me dear Christ"
HSSighs	"O might those sighs"
HSSouls	"If faithful souls"
HSSpit	"Spit in my face"
HSVex	"O to vex me"
HSWhat	"What if this present"
HSWhy	"Why are we by all creatures"
HSWilt	"Wilt thou love God"

Sigla for sources containing the Holy Sonnets

Group III mss. (early text)	B46	British Lib. ms. Stowe 961
	H5	Harvard U Lib. ms. Eng. 966.4
	HH1	Huntington Lib. ms. EL6893
	C9	Cambridge U Lib. ms. Add. 8468
	H6	Harvard U Lib. ms. Eng. 966.5
Group IV (intermediate text)	NY3	New York Public Lib., Westmoreland ms.
Group I mss. (later text)	B32	British Library ms. Harley 4955
	C2	Cambridge U Lib. ms. Add. 5778(c)
	C8	Cambridge U Lib. ms. Add. 8467
	O20	Bodleian Lib. ms. Eng. poet. e.99
	SP1	St. Paul's Cathedral Lib. ms. 49.B.43
Group II mss. (rev. later text)	B7	British Lib. ms. Add. 18647
	CT1	Trinity Coll., Cambridge, ms. R.3.12
	DT1	Trinity Coll., Dublin, ms. 877
	H4	Harvard U Lib. ms. Eng. 966.3
	WN1	National Lib. of Wales, Dolau Cothi ms. 6748

POEMS　　A (1633)　B (1635)　C (1639)　D (1649)　E (1650)　F (1654)　G (1669)

The Mirrour of Complements　　30 (1650)

Figure 2: Copies of Holy Sonnets in Seventeenth-Century Artifacts

Source	HSMade	HSDue	HSSighs	HSPart	HSBlack	HSScene	HSLittle	HSRound	HSMin	HSSouls	HSDeath	HSWilt	HSSpit	HSWhy	HSWhat	HSBatter	HSShe	HSShow	HSVex
AF1	•		•			•			•										
B6	•																		
B7		•	•	•	•	•		•	•		•	•	•	•	•	•			
B32		•	•	•	•			•	•		•	•	•	•	•	•			
B46	•	•	•	•	•	•	•	•	•	•	•								
C2		•	•	•	•	•		•	•		•	•	•	•	•	•			
C9	•	•	•	•	•	•		•	•		•	•	•	•	•	•			
CT1		•	•	•	•	•		•	•		•	•	•	•	•	•			
DT1		•	•	•	•	•		•	•		•	•	•	•	•	•			
H4		•	•	•	•	•		•	•		•	•	•	•	•	•			
H5	•	•	•	•	•	•	•	•	•	•	•								
H6	•	•	•	•	•	•	•	•	•	•	•								
HH1	•	•	•	•	•	•	•	•	•	•	•								
NY3	•	•	•	•	•	•	•	•	•	•	•	•	•	•	•	•	•	•	•
O20		•	•	•	•			•	•		•	•	•	•	•	•			
SP1		•	•	•	•	•		•	•		•	•	•	•	•	•			
WN1			•	•		•			•		•		•	•					
A		•	•	•	•	•		•	•		•	•	•	•	•	•			
B–G	•	•	•	•	•	•	•	•	•	•	•	•	•	•	•	•			
30	•	•																	

Figure 3

1633 Sequence (Siglum A)	1635 Sequence (Siglum B)	Previously un-printed sonnets (from ms.)	1639-1669 Sequence (Sigla C-G)
1 HSDue	HSMade ←———	1 **HSMade**	I. HSMade
2 HSBlack	1 HSDue	2 HSDue	II. HSDue
3 HSScene	HSSighs ←———	3 **HSSighs**	III. HSSighs
4 HSRound	2 HSBlack	4 HSPart	IV. HSBlack
5 HSMin	HSLittle	5 HSBlack	V. HSLittle
6 HSDeath	3 HSScene	6 HSScene	VI. HSScene
7 HSSpit	4 HSRound	7 **HSLittle**	VII. HSRound
8 HSWhy	HSSouls	8 HSRound	VIII. HSSouls
9 HSWhat	5 HSMin	9 HSMin	IX. HSMin
10 HSBatter	6 HSDeath	10 **HSSouls**	X. HSDeath
11 HSWilt	7 HSSpit	11 HSDeath	XI. HSSpit
12 HSPart	8 HSWhy	12 HSWilt	XII. HSWhy
	9 HSWhat		XIII. HSWhat
	10 HSBatter		XIV. HSBatter
	11 HSWilt		XV. HSWilt
	12 HSPart		XVI. HSPart

Figure 4

B-G + 18th- & 19th-c. editions	Grierson (1912)	Gardner (1952)	Shawcross (1967)	Smith (1970) & Patrides (1985)
I. HSMade	I. HSMade	1 HSDue	[1]	
II. HSDue	II. HSDue	2 HSBlack	[2]	
III. HSSighs	III. HSSighs	3 HSScene	[3]	revert to
IV. HSBlack	IV. HSBlack	4 HSRound	[4]	Grierson's
V. HSLittle	V. HSLittle	5 HSMin	[5]	order
VI. HSScene	VI. HSScene	6 HSDeath	[6]	
VII. HSRound	VII. HSRound	7 HSSpit	[7]	
VIII. HSSouls	VIII. HSSouls	8 HSWhy	[8]	
IX. HSMin	IX. HSMin	9 HSWhat	[9]	
X. HSDeath	X. HSDeath	10 HSBatter	[10]	
XI. HSSpit	XI. HSSpit	11 HSWilt	[11]	
XII. HSWhy	XII. HSWhy	12 HSPart	[12]	
XIII. HSWhat	XIII. HSWhat	**Sonnets added in 1635**		
XIV. HSBatter	XIV. HSBatter	1 HSMade	[13]	
XV. HSWilt	XV. HSWilt	2 HSLittle	[14]	
VI. HSPart	XVI. HSPart	3 HSSighs	[15]	
	XVII. HSShe	4 HSSouls	[16]	
added from NY3 {	XVIII. HSShow	**HSS from NY3**		
	XIX. HSVex	1 HSShe	[17]	
		2 HSShow	[18]	
Hayward (1929) and **Bennett** (1942) follow Grierson		3 HSVex	[19]	

Figure 5

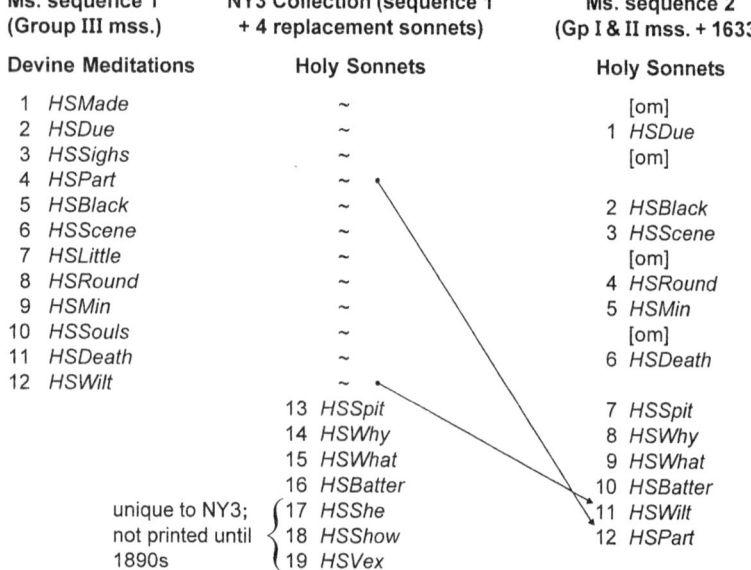

Ms. sequence 1 (Group III mss.) Devine Meditations	NY3 Collection (sequence 1 + 4 replacement sonnets) Holy Sonnets	Ms. sequence 2 (Gp I & II mss. + 1633) Holy Sonnets
1 HSMade	~	[om]
2 HSDue	~	1 HSDue
3 HSSighs	~	[om]
4 HSPart	~	2 HSBlack
5 HSBlack	~	3 HSScene
6 HSScene	~	[om]
7 HSLittle	~	4 HSRound
8 HSRound	~	5 HSMin
9 HSMin	~	[om]
10 HSSouls	~	6 HSDeath
11 HSDeath	~	7 HSSpit
12 HSWilt	~	8 HSWhy
	13 HSSpit	9 HSWhat
	14 HSWhy	10 HSBatter
	15 HSWhat	11 HSWilt
	16 HSBatter	12 HSPart
unique to NY3; not printed until 1890s {	17 HSShe	
	18 HSShow	
	19 HSVex	

Figure 6: Group IV (NY3) changes to Group III text

HSDue 12

Group III   Oh, I shall soone despaire, when I **shall** see
             That thou lou'st Man kind well, yet wilt not chuse me,

NY3   Oh I shall soone despayre, when I **do** see
             That thou lov'st Mankind well, yet wilt not chose me.

HSPart 14

Group III   Thy lawes abridgement, and thy last command
             Is all but Loue, Oh let **thy** last will stand!

NY3   Thy lawes abridgment, and thy last Command
             Is all but Love; Oh let **that** last Will stand.

HSLittle 13

Group III   And burne me, **o Lord**, with a firy zeale
             Of thee and thy house, which doth, in eatinge, heale.

NY3   And burne me, **o God**, with a fiery Zeale
             Of thee, 'and thy house, which doth in eating heale

HSSouls 14

Group III   . . . then turne
             (O pensiue soule) to God, for he knowes best
             Thy **griefe**, for he put it **into** my brest.

NY3   . . . then turne
             O pensiue Soule to God; for he knowes best
             Thy **true griefe**, for he put it **in** my brest.

HSDeath 8

Group III   And soonest our best men with thee doe goe,
             Rest of their **bodyes**, and Soules deliuery

NY3   And soonest our best men with thee do go,
             Rest of ther **bones**, and Soules deliueree.

Figure 7: Group I changes to Group III-IV text

HSPart 12

Groups III & IV   . . . let thy all-healing grace and spirit
             Reviue **and quicken**, What lawe and letter kill.

Group I   . . . But all-healing grace, and spiritt
             Reviue **agayne**, what lawe and letter kill,

HSBlack 5

Groups III & IV
             Or **as** a Theife, which till Deaths doome be read
             Wisheth himselfe deliuered from prison,

Group I   Or **like** a Theife, which till Deaths dombe bee redd,
             Wisheth himselfe deliuered from Prison

Figure 8: Group I revisions of the NY3 text in the replacement sonnets

HSSpit 3

NY3   For I haue sin'd, and sin'd: and **humbly** hee
                      Which could do no iniquity hath dyde.

Group I   For I haue sin'd, and sind, and **only** hee
                      Who could doe none Iniquitye, hath dyed,

HSWhy 1

NY3   Why **ame I** by all Creatures wayted on?

Group I   Why **are wee** by all Creatures wayted on?

HSWhy 9

NY3   **Alas I'ame weaker, wo'is me**, and worse then you,

Group I   **Weaker I am, woe ys me**, and worse then you.

HSWhat 8

NY3   And can that toung adiudge thee vnto hell
                      Which Prayed forgiuenes for his foes **ranck** spight?

Group I   And can that Tounge adiudge thee to hell,
                      Which prayed forgiuenes for his foes **fierce** spight?

Figure 9: The Group-II revision of the Group-I text

HSScene 7

Group I (and III, IV)
            And glottonous death, will instantlye vnioynte
            My Body, and soule, and I shall sleepe a space,
            Or Presentlye, I knowe not, see that face,
            Whose feare alreadye shakes my Euerye Ioynte

Group II
            And Gluttonous death will instantly vnioint
            My Bodie, and Soule; and I shall sleepe a space
            But my euer wakeing part shall see that face
            Whose feare alreadye shakes my Euerye Ioynte